Gordon Massman
The Essential Numbers
1991 - 2008

Gordon Massman

The Essential Numbers

1991 - 2008

TS PRESS
2009

Gordon Massman, The Essential Numbers 1991 -2008

First edition, May 2009
ISBN: 9780977901999
Printed and bound in the USA.
Library of Congress Control Number: 2008943581

Cover painting is Noah Saterstrom's *pontiff: visitation*, oil on canvas, 24" x 36," 2008
Text is in Jenson. Titles are in Jenson and Georgia.

Tarpaulin Sky Press
PO Box 189
Grafton, Vermont 05146
www.tarpaulinsky.com

For more information on Tarpaulin Sky Press perfect-bound and hand-bound editions, as well as information regarding distribution, personal orders, and catalogue requests, please visit our website at www.tarpaulinsky.com.

1711

So here you are in my room, so shove it up your ass mr. big shot,
skull & bones, scythe man, spider fingers wrapping big mouth
round lymph glands or brain matter, mr. infirm eater with gap-
ing jaw, haw haw haw, who's under your rustling cape but an
empty groin, hole for cock, coccyx kook, go pester elsewhere
the Chesterfield lung, the homicide's hypodermic ride, go fuck
yourself, I've eaten oatmeal enough to fill a lake and univer-
sities of fish, I shit every bloody day and hydrate like a drain,
drive a bucket of balls thrice every seven days, so blow it out
your ass, you've come for me, fine, be done with it, I joghead,
I weightpump, decapitate me then like a sour grapes cricket,
you fuckbutt, what do I care, you stink like a port-o-potty,
slit me, slip out my spine, flounder, bull red, speckled trout,
leave aplate the rotting white meat of me, butter soaked,
coagulate, head in the trash, after this freeze my sister like
a genital wart, snow her into the john or underpants, flecks
on flecks spotting the water, fall leaves, wet streets, tire tra-
cks on stuck yellow, with her ribs pick your teeth, blowhard,
I poke a finger through your noneyes, gossamer sockets dry
as bleached pelvises, meatless pig, I jack off in your sky-
wide mouth, boneless bones, electrical zero, collector of the
gorgeous impotent pathetically enhoused mortal valkeries.

1699

I have never loved anyone, not you Elizabeth, nor you Cynthia, nor you Betty Sue, I fucked you all but never loved you, I bought property with you but never loved, I fathered children with you but never loved, not you, not the babies, not the babies as teenagers or adults, I did not love Scottie that regal Afghan, Kimberly, I never loved you in your devotion, I invaded your body hundreds of times, ate you, watched you suck me, we came steady as pulses, but I did not love you, I usually stared abstractedly over your shoulder or relived some parental indiscretion or felt nothing but mechanical pleasure, friction, buildup, climax, to the dozens of women I sampled but rejected, hope was never yours, I presented you the illusion of loving you but I did not, I wanted to but did not, aware of others awaiting my seduction I dumped you with small remorse, like a fly bite it hurt, I recorded in poems like this indictment, it should not have surprised when the guillotine dropped, I am fifty-seven, bald, gray, appreciably fit, gelled, and suspect I shall die without bestowing love, women I am incapable of loving, men I despise, a concentrated emotion: I hate men, I hate their shoes, I hate their cellphones, I hate their slacks, I hate their cars, I hate their hair, I hate their rings, I hate their penises, I hate their toes, I hate their stupefying vapid tongue, I fantasize clocking men, opening fire on men, I refuse acknowledging the presence of men, rather I stare through them or ignore their existence, if I say hello I am thinking screw you, to me men fail, scooting butts forward against commercialism's kick, scheming and negotiating, absorbing into vampiric corporate labyrinths squandering the exquisite human potential on marketing techniques and implementation, sold down the river, defenseless and propagandized, the contemptible gender ground into fodder, troweled into graves by invisible hands, big shots, movers and shakers, unknowingly licked to the paper stick like dimestore suckers by diabolical tongues, tragic creatures lanced through heart and believing it fine, I never loved you Jean though we coupled on beaches, in hot tubs, and inside some Hawaiian cottage quieted by drizzle, hazel steel unblinking eyes gaped over your shoulder like a porcelain doll, I never groaned nor abandoned control, a textbook technician, man floating in jar of liquid, handsome, naked, smoothly muscled, formaldehyde riven ready for the scalpel-clutching, squeamish high school biology class dissection.

1692

Poetry the poison, poetry the lie, poetry the venom shot through rattler fangs, poetry the monster, the assassin, the embezzler, poetry the totalitarian, poetry the expired Mercurochrome dabbed on wound, poetry worm eaten wood, dead love, abandonment, poetry rabies slaughtered with the dog, poetry raw chicken stinking in sun on some Gulf pier no gulls swoop for, poetry the raped prepubescent, the assaulted grandmother, the beaten delivery boy, poetry collateral damage, poetry war, poetry death by friendly fire, poetry gangland murder of the snit, poetry the wasp sting while collecting mail, poetry the sweet carcinogen in Virginia Slims, poetry the mirage, the convection wave, the refracted post sticking out water, poetry pancreatic cancer, poetry lymphoma, poetry cancer of the throat and tongue, poetry the black plague reincarnated in universities, poetry staring as dysentery in the Ganges River, resultant diarrhea and death by dehydration, poetry the inactionable advertising campaign related to weight loss and hair replacement schemes, poetry silicone implants leaking into fat, poetry the sewing needle lodged in a dog's lower intestine, poetry penis pump surgically inserted like a rage balloon, the chemical compound in brain associated with sociopathology, poetry neither the force that drove spikes through palms nor the quintessence of Eve's naivete, but a simple gob of tubercular spit stringing off the filthy bar of a street grate.

1672

Bastard seeking bastardess, argumentative, defensive, unexamined fucker looking for same, bald, salt and pepper, 6'1" , uncommunicative, proud, stubborn, unbiblical, clean hands, rich, GTO, loathes his mother, despises Dad, whines and wheedles, insomniac, uses intimate partner for literary material, unabashed, premature ejaculator with virtuoso tongue, estranged from grown children, one cat, body dysmorphic dysfunction and OC-D, binge eater, Ben and Jerry's, cheese enchiladas, chocolate fudge, then wants to vomit on the cat, on anything, on breasts, prefers defeat, fantasizes knifing his cuddling lovers, their aggravating hands and French poodle squeals, fantasizes strangling or instantaneous suffocation, iron pumping gym rat, rigid, implacable, ultracontrolling, eschews mountains, hiking, skiing, camping, horses, dogs, motorcycles, roller blading, golf, single track, bedandbreakfasts, travel, board games, dancing, prefers sardonic fucking at sea level, piercing gull cries, the occasional pelican, obedience, frigid, non-orgasmic, comespitters need not apply, nor spirituality queens, nor unity freaks, nor, god help us, poets, prefers enraged, insatiable, pseudo-feminist slave, raw on the floor, ground beef, selfloathing, dry fallen debutante who disrelishes kids, a bloody Ambien addict, super-hyper-educated hair afire neurotic screaming catastrophe to catastrophe with water bucket and double scotch, me: slit from soul by the impalpable knife, you: masochistic, self-effacing, suicidal, insatiable, brilliant, murderous, with lips engaged in channeling excrutiating ecstasy capable of severing me from my genitals.

1670

Harrington practiced love till his face blued, then he shot someone pinking his mug back to normal pallor, screw Jesus he thought and stamped a bug flat as rice paper, yes, catharsis, cathexis of annihilation, brutality restores self, that frozen sirloin strip, thaws the cube in blowtorch rage prefatory to swallow and mastication, what idiot restores sight to blindness when he can gouge blindness from sight thereby creating from flaccid flesh sheer poetry, poetry of mutilation, poetry of war, poetry of combat and denigration, peace violence-sculpted into beauty, Achilles, Odysseus, Ajax, Agamemnon, every corpse a stanza, every war an epic, every century a collection exquisite, sublime, Harrington's wife would not shut up, he popped her, Harrington's son slumped, he shin-kicked him, Harrington found an old Louisville Slugger and redesigned some things, James Earl Ray and Sirhan Sirhan took down hope and compassion respectively, Gopal Godse took down love forming a sumptous triad of mastery, dominance, and durability, Jesus puttered like a lunatic around withered hands and epilepsy, a glove and a mouth-foamer akin to a vomiting frog, before the rhapsody of the crucifix brilliantly wrote him on timbers and nails, three incomparable co-authors, Judas, Pilate, Caiaphas, employing that most fabulous composer of immortal magnificence: hate.

1665

Men and women hate their lives, eye liner, shave cream, hemorrhoidal gel, and meat tenderizer combine into napalm; children equal agent orange; Meg would rather die. Arnold wants to gut people like trout; I love you seeps from exploded car batteries; god is a light bulb people burst inside their mouths and swallow, bloody bowels; the sewing needle my mutt ate tattooed hell onto his gut; Rog blew his head off with internet porn. bits splattered his silver phone; mostly Edward plods and trudges cursing his blasphemous biological ignoramuses, Gregor and Dawn, two gutless toadies; one gives birth to one's own electroshock treatments; Melvin bursts through the back door like a laxative commercial, 6:43 PM, maintains exuberance halfway down the hall before petrifying into a self-mocking sneer terminating in an unsuccessful episode on the toilet, the cutlets ready for ketchup and cheer; they watched the house go up, slab, frame, drywall, nails, bing bang bing bong, garbage disposal, house, three months, eleven days, twenty-seven minutes, brass keys; set up shop, dishes, pillows, stein collection, laundry soap pellets; somewhere, somewhere Charlie got left behind, stuck behind the sink plumbing with the can of Comet, somewhere, faraway Patty's legs walked away from her torso and continued walking into this house full of Tupperware; oh well; Sherman's company promoted him to assistant marketing manager; Sherman grasps the pay hike like a steel bar, no insubstantial benefits from prayer, for example, or spirituality; years ago Stephie's man ceased kissing, igniting a slow seething fire, she crisps the meat and morning yolks bleed, behind the blank screen CSI reels like a pinwheel; she sneaks schnapps, he scours Match.com; she craves sadistic men, gigantic cocks ramming up her rigged by rope, he imagines titanic tits, two to each girl, one sucking him off, the other's vagina squeezing his tongue, painted toe nails and pierced clits; the overdue feasibility study eats his soul's pink escargot; goddammit to hell the fucking bastards; Ginger's con-

quering the planet with Yale on the way, Cosmopolitan or Marie Claire;
Atkins sliced twenty pounds off her thighs; Ferragamo's sexes her soles;
God's finger scatters minnows, God bombs the pond, women scatter in
three dimensions, terrorist's nails lodge in strangers' entrails, the concussion
untwines lovers' intertwined fingers; nothing to be done, zilch to reconstruct.
designate someplace as home, go there, drink the stale air, consume your dinner.

1662

Men want to fuck God. Not women. God. Women are merely pale substitutes. Men want immortal fucking, fucking extra-human, the creator of women. Nothing short of that. Jennifer or Diane can make him come but not like God. God makes him come beyond mortality, beyond dissatisfaction. God does not have perfect feet, like Rebecca, manicured and polished, but has blinding feet, impossible to glimpse, incomparable feet made of white hot light. God does not have mere voluptuous breasts with upturned nipples made of fat and glands. God's breasts envelope the world, deliver the death of discontent, death of feeling. Anything short of that is just Megan or Klarissa with moles or bruises but will do in emergencies. Lisa's body bracketed by pate and soles, visible in one click, sixty-three inches tall, bracketed by air, falling through air like a dropped lake pebble, nothing, impotent, insignificant. God encompasses oceans and, therefore, must be fucked by men. Men yearn. God eludes. Men push through Carolyn reaching for God. Cocks cry milk tears. Men hate their women for not being God and weep out the back door like refugees. A lizard. A flowering tree. Another clay substitute. A dark hammer. He extracts Betty's heart like a hairless puppy and somewhere plants it. What grows looks nothing like God.

1643

I create god in my image, he's deluded in acknowledging me, you possess my soul, I say, my spirit, life everlasting is yours, you shall worship me and sanctify sacred holidays—Michaelmas, Palm Sunday—you shall compose a scripture and liturgy, practice humility and obey commandments forbidding all sins emblazoned on granite tablets, you shall kneel before me, cover your pate, read daily the holy sacrament, mutter "father", "lord", "king", "omniscient one", "door Massman", through me shall you receive immortality though you are stiff-necked and narcissistic, a worm with vengeance to chop in two, cur to drown, inconsequential beast though I number your every pore, I create you now with toenail clippings, pubic hairs, pennies and toothbrush bristles, bang!, god, bang! daddy, bang! ring-leader, my menial slave sacrificing animals with the long bladed knife and flaming votives like a pyromaniac, I can drop you in vat or crash your Chevrolet, I have already programmed the extermination of your son by a date specific and inescapable: suicide by financial ruination exacerbated by marital stupidity—a prima donna wife, a frigid queen—he shall blow out his heart, inescapably, like a fool in an infinite line of fools, your first increase splattered across a bluebonnet field, I construct you with my jaw bone, erection, posture, width, my Russian complexion, a flawless speller and raging regimentarian, while you sleep this night I will stuff your borrowed brow with mountain laurel and vine and you shall awaken in depthless incredulity craving brownish-yellow wine, my tour-de-force, my wunderkind, swifter than mercury, in likeness of me, now I survey my population: pornographers, hypergraphias, counterfeiters, bums, crowding like a clot of maniacs, my condemned bewildered supplicants teeming in a pile of nourishment, from on high, cloud-enthroned, magnificent, omnipotent, gorgeous, bounteous I with wrist-flick ejaculate you after which sutures, semen, spikes, nails, and dust fuse into a murderous mass of uninhabitable flesh.

1635

I pray for myself, my anger, my compulsion to ruin, how I dive slippery from the womb of love, swan-like, my rage stinking of storage bins, oh Lord, with awe and humility, peaceable habitation, unalterable decrees, how humanity disgusts, festering acid-filled sore of steering wheels and stupidity, uneducated squabbling thugs with cash wads and pistols, I participating in its vortex, contemptuous father-loather crammed in funnel like a doomed dunce, fly into me a seraphim, oh Expiator, coring hell from me, brass knuckled fantasies showering blows upon a driver at his car window or shoving mr. cock against gym lockers, naked, bursting nose, a male bellicosity crossed into psychopathology, reptilian rivals beaded on desert rocks, O Benevolent Intercessor, Cedars-Sinai Medical Center, Barnes Jewish Hospital, St. Luke's Presbyterian, they give you new hearts, clashing scalpels and bang! you're spinning sequins of revelation, suck Prominent One, my bulb free of scorpions, that I may meet camaraderie in hairy testicles and blue shaved faces splashed with fucking and Menen bracer for men are one glueball of love, dear Heavenly Doctor, roll up my sleeve, locate muscle, pump in relaxation, selflessness, luminescence, humility, fellow-feeling.

1624

First we plunge knife into dog, she fell to knees, toppled, lay
like any meal in gravy, spotted tongue, then baby Lulu, thirt-
een months, pillow over face, pressure, turkey before baking,
extracted pussy by back legs from cabinet, beheaded him,
whole head glued to chair like shish kabob, marinated head-
less body in loggy toilet bowl, you sliced my clothes like
gutting fish, whack whack cling, strips, I lopped your bras
for mastectomy, slashed French panties like jelly crea-
tures, we eyed each other, "love," you said, "love," I assented,
"screw you," you said, "agreed," I chimed, "I despise your
mother," "yours drank herself dead," "None will adore
you like me," she warned, "Echo," I responded, one by one
we pulled the feathers off Dante our Parrot, poor Dante
caged and fruited like a bauble, several primary feathers
plucked killed him like a shot weight, claws clutching a
finger, "monster," she screamed, "Frankenstein," I fired,
"piece of shit," shot out the canon my mouth, bereft
of pets and babies her wishbone glittered like a lit ship-
sail, meathooks, striations, bruise red bloomed in my
mind, psychopath, maniac, she studied me like a cannibal,
and down we tumbled in a flurry of slurp, boner, juice,
and squish, slacks and shirts collapsing like parachutes.

1618

I masturbate to fashion photos of anorexics, Auschwitz ladies hips crooked outward slathered in blue cotton panties, elbow pelvises, furrows and funnels, cheeks like eaten stone, imagine fucking grasshopper bodies so close it rubs bone, wire sculpture of horror harboring a wet pussy, I bend coathanger legs around my neck, twist feet together, have at her, cupping her forkhandle spine, spit into her, lick metal, pierce her bubble eyes dripping off magnesium strips like screams, fold back the page and hammer hammer my fat grotesque sunless white apparition, stuff soft batch into maw and jack myself off like a wedge of bacon, this sick self-induced holocaust conductor, acid on acid, cur rib, sexy speck of death, pubis stuck up like a popped firecracker, cupped Sahara leaf-tongue, gold braceleted, bronzed, delectable razor edge crying for danger, murder, castration, breakage, thimble pederast tits with big nipples, I'm baked and splitting, steaming and falling open, like thick brisket, hissing, fire red, barbecue splendor, American male tangled in carbon smudges and cocaine, invidious envier sniffing up Andrea's cunt and Jennifer's butt, slim as paperclips and screaming all night for butter lumps, I papercut my shaft against her last gasp minutes before the bulldozer's blade.

1615

Bugs fly off hand when I brush my arm: fleas, chiggers, thrips, weevils burst into clouds, die, crawl in waves; neck disintegrates into fruit flies, eaten, ravaged such as months of decomposition in wet soil, lice lift off my face like leprosy, re-land and devour, lips glisten with the wings of roaches, I belch a mosquito cumulus cut by rays, beautiful black ball orange-suffused, toenail ticks, millipedes, mayflies, covered in microscopic dung, I shit compactions of spider, horsefly, larvae, emerald phosphorescence plopped in water, well, I deplore you, your cowboy moustache, your gut, your nasty cigarettes, big jewelry, and sandy bouffant hair, butt flicker and language hack, I deplore human beings spitting foul yellow juices into gutters and eating mercilessly like vats of acid, swagger and braggadocio, beefy men plowing furrows into concrete, well, fuck my hostility, I masturbate a colony of squash bugs, I sit, invariably, upon my thick pit of silverfish ass. . . .

1613

First I razor free my mouth, lips make a thick rubber band. Second I slice round the perimeter and peel off nipples, piña colada umbrellas. Third, I exacto-knife toadstool tip of penis, lift it off, the pee-slit forms a lovely salt shaker. Sections of me rehabilitate the house: sphincter muscle, ear lobes, esophagus, gall bladder toilet floater. I exhaust my body parts. A heart, a cardiovascular system wound round spine upright in a chair, eyes gaping mid-air. Love energizes the liquor cabinet. Anger bubbles porridge. Cartilage strengthens window cranks. Smooth muscle revitalizes Beautyrest. I have nothing to offer weather stripping, sputtering sidearm, I'm all in, my stretched back skin approximates wallpaper, oh I flipped for her, I landed on my edge, I sucked her in through a hydrodynamic straw, no crab this, awkwardly scuttling across concrete slab, ticking like asphyxiation, we're fork knife and spoon, split peas and water, sauerbraten medallions beside potato salad, godfuckingdamn, I popped off kneecap like the whacked open top of a monkey skull, shut it over pot of boiling god, oh Patty Sue, my tendons work the living room blinds which blot out eyes like a terrorist's knotted rag. Here's my book, *The Devil's Carnival of Body Parts and Love*, slip it on like shoes, drain it through neck, blow bubbles into it like a warm soapy sponge. Last, I saw upward through the crack in my ass creating two Brahma dewlaps, one a bucket of grease to gouge fingers into, one a bursting piñata laden with candy.

1603

Dear mother, murder daddy, kill yourself, fill the house with blood,
bleed your red nails into his skull like ten Esterbrooks, those sexy
wet nails, through his Ambien induced unconsciousness empty your-
self soaking his bed like a Kotex, pad to the kitchen in your pink
chiffon nightie and support hose, slide the drawer, remove the butch-
er knife, whisper back down the Florida green carpet to this room,
stand a while, then jam it in, the mattress soaking life, draining
to box spring, his lipless mouth opening like a sea shell, the deed
done return to your scalloped black boudoir and down the alcohol
river of pills, the two dead humans of 425 Miramar, Corpus Christi,
TX., Dear mother, scrub the grime of hate off your tub, the filth of
bitterness from the toilet bowl, your bathroom stinks, it breathes
rage, clean the crusted cave in one heroic act, that foul porcelain
urn in which you have shit and bathed for eighty years, your life.
I fantasized fantasizing spooning Gerber's into your mouth, veal
and peas, finding sparks in your long gray hair, and lifting daddy
like a madonna off his sheets, stuffing his mouth with your
hair to bind you, your toes in his, an eternal loop, instead this:
once in neck, once in chest, once in groin, a fourth and fifth
in chest again, split your legs like Alaskan crab, a house with-
out lungs, with larynx removed, lake flat tongue filling the
gullet, elephant collapsing to front knees, collapsing again af-
ter standing, rolling to right shoulder, smack, pillars obscene-
ly crossed as if loafered, oh mommy rationalize, planet, ice age,
mastodon, who gives a shit, geological time, 83, 86, embez-
zlement, crushed Chevrolets, Max Factor, Revlon, Maybel-
line emptied, plowed under, glass to sand, Edie, Sylvan, Julius
dank ulnas and fibulas, dead your great great grandchildren's
grandchildren, necks split like baked apples, Saturn, sun, the

farthest frozen reaches, cold rage, cold life, frozen flames,
both hands over head, the man is already dead, your slam-
ming door cut your babies' umbilical chords, gaze on him,
with calculated abandon plunge plunge plunge plunge plunge.

1599

Lambs and apologies, humility and shame, self-effacement, lowering of eyes and diminution, the soap of absolution, the tongue held out for bitters and ash, the goose pimply flesh of shuddering leaves, Michelangelo babies, wind-billowed sheets on coastal clothes line, all blood stays in veins, lanolin, shovels and pails, cherubic births and milky nipples, milk itself poured from glazed pitchers, mothers nearby in sails of flesh, fish soft as a woman's belly and rosy feet dripping tub water in white light, roast chicken and cranberries, green beans almandine, prayer and health, "God bless this table and friends," pink bows and blue and Mickey Mouse waffles, dog vacuuming dirt on the scent of game, bruisy clouds cracking a clear smile through abating gloom, immense square teeth and pillowy lips, gold fields awash in dusk speckled with crows and dark nuggets, mother serves brisket to her seated family: gee mommy this is good, and mashers too!, with a stack of pre-sliced bread, and afterward 'nana pudding with 'Nilla Wafers, seconds, please, oh sweetie, bedtime stories all round, a palm on the forehead—no fever, knock on wood—and a kiss night-night, Chevy sleeps beside Ford, birdcage covered, chains latched for extra protection, and lawns get their crowns of dew, gradually, as the all night president in the only illuminated room in night's gut-pit shields his sleeping children against doom, robins swoop on morning's threads and little holes cough up rabbits, look, a bunny!, daddy bursts yolks with toast, kiddies get coco puffs, to school with lunch money and shoes; patriotism, altruism, troop 218, Henry "Hank" Josephs, scoutmaster, of the Lincoln Memorial, awe, the Washington Monument, awe, awe the Treasury Department and apple blossom time, subservience, self-negation, penitent, a pie for Mrs. Kendenhall, bow thy paltry head, common laborer, humble servant, foot solider of the law, oh honey baby, nondescript condominium of worthlessness.

1598

I pretend you're a fraud; when I pray I say, "dear fucker who doesn't exist," under lids eyes flutter, "dear shitface, save a kid, do something," praying, though hypocrite, fake, silence ought to rein, the void before sleep or slippers, not this, "dear huckster, make baby well," petitions for health, prosperity, longevity, therefore I'm indoctrinated, theistic, shepherded, I pray for atheism, dear curtainman step outside, show me your lie, he remains sequestered in an invisible closet working levers, printing prayerbooks, composing hymns, denying me diploma or courage, so I pray dear freaking charlatan bastard sonofabitch, "don't crash us," "find me a mate," "kill his craving," you lousy goddamn fake which I can't disprove, bake me a marble cat's eye blue, round sturdy glass, cooked in red flame, into my lap drop it, filled with atheism.

1597

I flip it upside down and squeeze the honey bear over my bald head,
I empty a 1-lb bag of refined sugar over the honey, I smear Smuck-
ers chocolate fudge across my chest and midriff, I empty jelly jars
onto my knees, strawberry knee, apricot knee, sprinkles everywhere,
I putty my belly button with Skippy, I sit in milk, I roll in pastry flour,
I smash a Nutty Buddy against my lips, I unwrap Snickers, Milky
Way, Mallow Cups and mash them into ears and anus, I pour Mrs.
Butterworth's down my spine, I stand in buckets of maple syrup, I
decapitate a dog and tie its face to my dick, I suck the ink from a
Bic, up my nose I shove gummy worms, everywhere nonpareils, I
squeeze wedge of frozen wedding cake between fingers, I snow
coconut slivers over God, now the dangling: snowballs from el-
bows, Twinkies from lobes, from ankles tails of naked Entenmann's,
Cinnebon from lower tooth, Double Stuff from ring knuckle, I
stand by fire, Bananas flame, hair flames, genitals flame, Yahweh
twirls me up through drums of cotton candy, bee hive, body beard,
cloaked to toenails, the dog's head bundled like a pork loin in
Saran Wrap, I pull a Tootsie Pop out my ass and flip it to a
child, an angel blesses me with a tongue of black molasses, oh
god, forgive him his self-inflicted sins, by a knot in the chord
clamped between teeth, I am lowered through the big top,
drums, harsh light illuminates my pores, into the middle ring.
I pay thirteen trained baboons to hose me down with popcorn.

1570

Hi, I'm Gordon, I'm a sex addict, hello, Gordon, I've been sex free for two days, thanks to my higher power, this morning I awoke, broke at the knees at bedside, prayed for strength, asked forgiveness, begged really, began to take an inventory of those I've wronged, sex nearly killed me, I've eaten asphalt, been hospitalized, lost family, friends, had a gun to my head, been fired multiply, eaten poison, terrified women, been imprisoned, and spent six weeks in rehab, this disease for that is what it is, this disease, this soul decay, only God can heal, God dusts off the fallen, the perniciously erect, the cunt chaser, the juice eater, in His infinite authority, I gave myself over, crossed my wrists, said dear Lord take me, do with me what you will, the exquisite blood-filled wet tight grotto, fuck, fuck, fuck the most beautiful word in the English language, fucking women, asses stuck up like jelly pots entered from the rear, fucking them on couches or floor, in chairs, with toys and thongs, pumps in air, I broke at knees, said, please please dear God I can't take it anymore, I'm dead, save, nipples, breasts, upward pointing, toes like heroin, arches, ridges, asses, breath, surrender, earthquake coming, when they arch upward, slave slave, master, fuck me, I love your cock might be heaven in language, cock, circumcision ridge flaring with urgency like the edges of earth, dear God destroy me, dear Being smite me for I am cruel, I am fucked up, I am bloody from masturbation, I am contaminated, when one squeezes me in her mouth, me over her head, watching me appear and disappear in her mouth, her mouth formed to succor me, thirsting for come, my bush at her nose, my clean shaft free of hair, I could die, I could die, die like a dead horse, an elegant dead stallion between her lips with my finger in her cunt, I'm Gordon, I'm an addict, I stand before you two days pure, reborn in the lamb of God, saved, almost deceased, hard even now behind this podium, but cognizant, wise, aware of the rod's destructive tendencies in the cesspool of desolation.

1562

Dear God, I wish to register my unhappiness about a few things: mortality is a crock of shit, I could pop you in the mouth for that; genocide sucks, you deserve a penitentiary gang raping; what about cerebral palsy? hanged by the neck, my good man, hanged by the neck; I'm a little discontent about mashed teenager canon-fodder wars, you know, blown off limbs and heads , amputated appendages, post traumatic stress syndrome, freckled unwrinkled babies mudtrudging, one could fucking kick you in the gonads or plier them off like taffy and feed 'em to chickens, here chick chick, you celestial amateur, scratchy violinist botching Bach; the little matter of pederasty, the constitutionally sour buggering preadolescents, or fucking itself between consenters whipping themselves leeward-to-stern chasing that momentary dopamine-filled squiggle infusing emptiness shame hunger megalomania and finally spiritual death, smashed in the kisser, banished, bibles burned simultaneously like flushing at once a skyscraper of toilets, bloody nutcase; what about space travel, you serve up famine, they booster to moon in million dollar foil suits to tramp around, demigods to television applause, famine's worth decapitation, (I assume neck not in ass a blade can find); oh boy peanut brickle Lucky Charms Mars AIDS Coke, finger-poke out your eye, sanctuary fornicator, superstition wrapped in faith wrapped in fear, Mr. Potato Head; I'll praise you this; blood-covered morsels ceaselessly bursting, new beautiful victims.

1561

I loathe myself down to my orange toenails; my bald dome, my sex addiction, my clumsiness, cherry juice splattering cabinets, obsessive-compulsive rituals twisting me like God, excessive defecation, urination fixation, numbers, locks, I hate my fat binge-weary gut stuffed simultaneously with burritos, corn chips, Velveeta con queso, refried beans, avocado, Spanish rice, pulled chicken, sopaipilla, honey, mint candy, ice cream, hot fudge, whipped cream, marshmallow, peanuts, iced tea, shredded spoonfuls, milk, slivered almonds, and artificial sweetener, a cauldron of garbage topping off my throat, I hate self-induced nausea and self-destruction, cunnilingus with victims and a hot shooting thread, she straddling he three fourths up her cunt in a wooden chair, masturbation-fascination and ensuing disgust, slice me like a hard boiled egg slicer, I hate every strip, bum, idiot, bungler, fucker, liar, fake, and fool, my pathetic decomposed lettuce leaf poetry, wet heavy stink, like uninterred flesh. "I hate my-self down to my orange toenails," for example, shit beside Seamus Heaney or Joseph Brodsky, shit beside even Nicholas Christopher and he's an idiot, terror of lonelin-ess, islanded by emptiness, a bloody untouched peninsula careening onto internet dating or prostitution, something foams doglike, something cracks its muzzle, something drains disease into its ears, head back, howling love love, something driven to shove it in hates carnality's whipping motion, the shoulder-to-butt hump, the embryo squish, how insomnia can-opens the top of my head, chef boy-ardee, three successive sleepless nights grabbing fistfuls of worms wriggling between fingers, oh god, abhorrence, hypercriticism, shiny cracker jacks spilled out a wrist, 2 frozen silhouettes rooted to a field, the children, distant, blocking sun, guilt-ridden, stilted, rejected them in self-absorption, incapable of simple medicinal restoration.

1560

Today I will die for a cause, infinitesimal defines my existence, indispensable the cause, I awake, I breathe, I straighten my uniform, it will be a magnanimous day, explosions, men clenching jaw, scarlet contorted, heroically grunting, the platoon one beautiful many-headed organism, I accept fate, God decreed that I pave the way with gore, others' bloody boots marching up my spine toward Jericho, today I will learn the melting point of bone and dissolve in the sky like a Sweet Tart, it's a seminal day, a parade-perfect day, clean, enormous, chattering rainbird sprinklers, the resurrected drowned stirring in slippers, glory's my song and death my gratitude, brylcream boots, oh baby I'll explode like outrushing semen among the crows and wrathful soldiers on this God-magnificent day of the continuous victory.

1557

A window washer slides down the slanted diamond-shaped skyscraper's roof, ripping fingernails prefatory to a five-hundred foot free fall to concrete below, an inconsequential human tearing gelatin on useless window frames, bursting mastodon heart, tool belt like train wheels striking metal strips clackety clackety clack, then, hands applauding air, the swan dive off the edge past advertising agencies, law firms, physicians' offices, employment agencies, brokerage businesses, investment concerns, the CEO seducing his marketing director, Cup-o-Soup containers on mahogany desks, a dismissal, plummeting package of a man plunging, no time for forgiveness or gratitude, just emergency images like a spiraling contrail, a woman not conjured in years, scoutmaster Hank, transformer toys, blizzard torn by wind, this Catholic stalwart and his morality, no extramarital affairs, no substances, Sunday pot roast and services, descending through hell like the bloody antichrist or some defeated science fiction monster, tail blowing upward, some justice, involuntary reflexes working to the end, the headline 6-pages deep in tomorrow's City Section already written: Stone Container Bldg. Window Washer Falls to Death.

1553

What have I done, I've murdered it, it was easy, spontaneous rage,
easy as smashing a vase or punching holes, but this time I've snuffed
life, I reach shudderingly in slanted shadow, to touch, to worship
the dead pile, blood spilled out its eye, I can't see damage to vital
organ, only evidential hemorrhaging, lethal blunt force, could I have
snapped the chord, in murdering it I murdered two, they will find,
convict, consign me to maximum, I'm the obvious suspect, a his-
tory of flashpoints, its companion of twenty years under same
freakin' roof, an irreversibly backlashed life, I always believed
that one day I would kill, the conditions volatile as the primordial
soup, calmly I sit, I expect no mercy in this culminating ejaculation,
the thick tap root blossoms its branches, there it lies, the registry
of my rage, buckled, contorted as if thrown from a windshield,
sphincter relaxed, peaceful at last, our fusion's summation, me
muttering, "I love you." "I didn't mean it." "We were wonderful."

1548

Mr. Knuckles worked me over, I passed out from shock proving I'm fragile protoplasm like any jellyfish, ever seen the cabbagehead washed up on shore, pathetic squashable bulb, Mr. Knuckles frustrated, self-loathing, not copulating, business failure, stringy boxer legs, long arms, nimble and dangerous, take that, he snapped and punched out an eye, worthless bum he yelped, and frankly I was a derelict, a foot dragger, self-conscious to paralysis, me observing me observing me observing like dueling mirrors, I the weaker, he the paragon, flunky, lazyass, dumb, and frankly I bombed out of trig and scraped by Spanish, school tumbled me through air backward like a bomb, he boffed my ears, big shot, he barked, he mashed my head to resemble a turd and flushed it down, take that cologne boy, (gushing water), I never touched him, I chewed double bubble, butch waxed wave, sugary smelling, you know, filled with Jackie DeShannon, kicked a notch into my shin, sloucher, I knew his avaricious discontent wife, knew her down to her Kotex, princess materialism w/ mortality complications, but forgave him not, my torturer risen from door-shadows, the hammer, haywire Judah Maccabee, paranoid of Nazis, acid spitter; now osteoporotic brittle baby, six inches shorter, I lift him like an empty Talis to his sagging throne, urine and excrement Tided out repeatedly, threadbare ermine sheets from yore, scepter as walker, head blotched eggplant purple, fists that pummeled saggy as scrotums.

1541

[I want to thank you for what you did back there] [you'd do the same] [but still you didn't have to] [it was reflex, it's hard wired, it's what's required out here, you know, alone out here] [okay, but thanks, thanks a lot, I owe you one] [you owe me nothing, I don't like you, I did it because I *had to*, that's all, had to not *want to*, if the tables were turned you'd do the same, even though I disgust you, same as me, out here we depend on each other, we need your back, your shoulders, I don't care what you did a month ago or a year ago, history doesn't exist here, here it's survival, man against that, that fucking shit out there, all of it, big indifferent shit, forget it, boss wants a tight ship, he gets a tight ship, no screw ups, no squabbling] [you could have let me go to the devil, no one would of blamed, you risked it all, I won't forget] [look out there, nothing but barrenness hostility ice death, incomprehensible hatred, we're two of a kind, mister, linked as if shackled, you die, I suffer, I die, you suffer, get it, we don't have to like each other, God doesn't give a shit about compassion, it's calculation fitness mimicry deception, if I didn't need you, right now, if you didn't fit into my immediate plan, I would have let it devour and shit you like crap through a fish, like an hour of sustenance given to the thing, that's why I saved you]

1526

God the sissy, God the playground joke-butt bul-
lies pummel, eating sod, spurting nose blood, kicked,
tripped, sniffling mommy, mommy but mommy's
gone on glue, hallucinating excuses and mastur-
bating rainbows, god's book satchel full of psycho-
drama, monsters, anxiety, incontinence, dodging
Ulrich and McGee, Jewboy, Jewboy they shout
and shove him down stairs, spreadeagle, papers
everywhere, Ulrich's German, Magee's Czech,
both with sadistic domineering dads in lower in-
testinal realms, biceps like boulders, Ulrich wedged
fingers between Varney's lips and ripped his
mouth apart, God's smart as crap, philosophies
like galaxies swirl his head, burdensome grandi-
osities pulling him topheavy like a power-drunk
nutcase involving punishments and holocausts,
sucking up in outspread arms oceans of heretics
and mimickers, McGee struck God like a kitchen
match, lighting afire His hair and spinning him
madly, laughter all round the lockers and shower
stalls, I'll create prison, God thought, invisible
barriers, stinking john, crawling with bugs,
windowless, cold for the fuckers, and so he did.

1523

This is me, here's my face, like a potted daffodil, brilliant, beautiful,
I crave love, I crave validation, my photo screams to distinguish
me, world traveler, beach comber, film aficionado, favorite cuisine:
French Provencal, recent book: The Secret Life of Bees, lattes at
Starbucks, candle-lit dinners, authenticity a must, notice my lux-
uriance pulls one toward it to finger and part, notice my Mediter-
ranean lips—two truant schoolgirls—exuberant, sweet, rebellious,
virginal, I own the sloop, that turquoise is Belize, the pussy's name:
Marmalade, rarely climax, "repressed," distrust strangers, love gard-
ening, experiments with razors, bubble baths, others have failed
my stringent test, all yours but deliver, perform as demanded, al-
most bit a dick in half, electroshocked father, creased upper lip,
sable mom, cultured black pearls, discovered tranquility be-
hind daddy's face, words aching to speak: "darling," "precious
darling," to cherish man to darling, this is me, perky, tan, tight—
a birthlook—head resplendent upon its stem, hungry caverns yearn-
ing for you, waterfall hair, c'mon look, dimestore playmate, un-
derneath *chic* raven black web—god's navel—nude pink nails,
honey-drenched knees, alternative spirituality, Pisces, look babe,
don't scratch too deep, I bleed envy, rage, spite, cruelty, schaden-
freude, when chemo fried Melissa hair secretly I rejoiced, desire
me, require me, baby, sweetiepie, I never loved Fascists, zealots,
or psychos, select me, I'm your on-line dream, over me spread
your stiff-beamed aphrodisiac: money, power, violence, invincibility.

1519

When they pry apart a man's arms and nail him by the wrists exposing him to weather, insects, adoration, whores, execrations, a person could mount and fellate the man while he gushes round nails, chest flung out, one could defile him with spray paint and lip gloss, our petty reprobate hammered tight, it's elementary math, some blathering lunatic hammered on a crucifix, an entomologist's butterfly, helpless against pederasts, rapists, winos, blacksmiths, swine, whose hearts and spit are unceremonious, all night stars yammer at the crucified: extortionist, megalomaniac, thief, murderer, fool out for ill-gotten gain, you pay sociopathology's price: ridicule, extinction, ignominy, you fuck with people you get screwed, it's law, it's a helluva way to fly, dead crosses cluttering the countryside but it beats vivisection, gives one a chance at rectification, some extra hours to utilize, and as I said, with chest protruding, arms flung out you never know what weird bullshit might rush in.

1507

I step toward dissolution, casting money like wallpaper strips, a dining room set, lamps, an antique wardrobe, I purchase a ticket to Cabo, dine at Geronimo (the baked helix escargot, the Maverick Ranch filet, the cappuccino semifreddo), float bloated to my Quattro, I'm over my cliff, bereft of mortgage, divorced, clientless, free of razor and cream, approaching filth, siphoning my check book a gasoline vandal, I philanthropize derelicts, my Wells Fargo petrol slurped to metal, gladly, a broker-boy AWOL, over the fence, clopping through mud in half-moonlight unhelmeted, illuminated by fired flare, fuck you, I yell, and peel a century note for a stranger, my parents' skeletons, bent, screaming, edematous, pasty, demented, my dog gone begging, my fingernails crab-ragged, my father's toenails curled like glue, I plant my lips on penury, suck out its lungs, spit into sea, lamprey, devastation's ecstasy, disgorging what one's earned, accumulated, and believed in chunky mess on clean terrazzo mainlines nirvana, sweet baby, better than vodka or Roy Rogers boots, I tell you unequivocally I splurge at Best Buy, appliances, electronics wiping out my Wachovia and am pure disgust, a lowlife, a terror-image, I mutter at myself execrables, son of Joseph, Abraham, and Jacob, cultivated, groomed, preselected, crawling into the spiteful glee of destitution.

1501

Testimony of the best pig in the sty. I'm king mounter. I shove it in. Gertrude craves me. Matilda moans for me. I grunt and eat slops pushing away others. I get mash. Dark splotchy pink, stout nose, neckless, number 77 tagged to left ear, luckiest number around. Rump like a cement mixer nobody kicks, squiggly firm tail, blood to tip. Super Pig, pig literati, nineteen-hundred twenty-six pounds, hog literally, the Indiana hogs, borne of Chester and Duchess, Chester Iowa State Fair Champion Derby Hog, Duchess six hundred pound 4-H Purebred Champion, daddy shot me into her like a roman candle. I burst forth like Ben Hur. Sunburnt from so much fucking, out from mud, into mud, ear tag jangling like revolutionary, Illini nights reclining under stars, contemplatively smoking, pink eyelids, lavish lashes, back legs crossed, I love everything, fences, twigs, friendship, water trough, soft breezes drawing across skin, the smell of piss, I, Davy Crockett pig, adventuresome, undaunted, courageous, proud, out to farthest post, to gate, scratching along wire, sniffing earth-untrodden, snorting intoxication-liberation, left-and-right pig, pig of The Nation and The New Republic, chest-out puffed-up herd-guardian wise warrior pig, pugnacious purple irremovable squealer.

1495

Dearest god, veal, my female genital, sweet silk pillow,
outline me in charcoal, reveal me, make me into para-
sol of oversweet blossoms, redeemer, overflower, I give
you the top half of two monkey skulls, my kneecaps,
yarmulkes baby lord for your bald wise head, I give you
three teeth, incisor, molar, bicuspid dangling in my
scrotum like spare rare jewels for your ancient gums,
please appreciate whom this prayer issues from—dy-
ing leaves, tattered fishmonger's shirt—that I may love
one entity, garbage cat, cloud horse, mountain lump,
my consolation beyond avocado dips, give me earth-
worm, slug, stink bug, anything gorgeous to recognize
like a brillo over burnt crud, our psalmists sang their
deathless songs, send me duiker, capybara, wildnymph
fawn that I may die into softness, make me irresistible.

1485

the monsters bent and demented, male wearing brown slippers shuffling to potty, lungless muscleless female stuck in bed like an old pudding, monsters once with farts like earthquakes and tongues like blunt instruments, now sallow losers dribbling special k milk and begging for help, not bankrupt, just ashamed, they horrify, these two juiced and squeezed, death egging on them like a botfly, what rot to multiply in, gross organic garbage, i love all things ruined to ineffectuality, weak as disease, i love them verging toward expiration, i powerful as gunpowder, shellacked by gyms, towering colossus beside their atrophied processes, oh time's cocktail disturbs me, but i'm in the powerful middle full-facultied like a staffed university and shall not be fear-crippled like these two defunct vicious possums. well, fuck it, i'm a calloused self-hating bastard. perceiving it, baby divorced me. knowing it, glo bolted. i shine inside assisted care facilities. oh sweetie lay me down among the incapacitated and watch me sleep the sleep of the glorious.

1483

This time, God, i'm humble, i want eternal everlasting, i repent on knobby knees my whoring, drugging, i was self-medicating with what felt fine, women, coke, oblivion, i ruled the world between legs or needle jab, i loathed daddy, that pig, that ungodly swine debasing innocence, humiliator, i fantasized axing him like seasoned pine, i'm done with rage, the man's childhood sucked, i love him now, trench mates horror filled, ole Jake's guts everywhere, we've witnessed hell, so i'm down, God, begging, forgive, exonerate, sanctify, cause me to vomit on ground, quaver with chills, make me swim in seas of bile, i am wicked, punish, wife me to condyloma, infested wart woman, i shall treasure her, utter gratitude on broken knees by our rotted bed-box, i have shamed, i have sat in what hate shat, reeked like anti-perfume, have articulated internally accusations, "big shot," "fuck head," "asshole," "lunatic" to male bystanders, never domitable, while worshiping females, so give me lymphoma, colitis, or dyspeptic ulcers that i may rip in me a portal through which you take up dwelling domicile and out which flows transgression like a slit sack of maggots.

1481

He ceased to eat for he wishes not to be one who eats, hunched over plate, fork afist, gut and hunger, commonplace, ordinary, until ceasing to eat he felt blasphemous eating, like a sinner, a dupe, bald head leaning into meat, tearing broccoli shoots, masticating, vapidly swallowing until voiding plate of all but grease, flotsam, residue, like craps table littered with scraps after game, he pours down throat quickset concrete and trowels shut his ass, and since you must know plugs nostrils and piss hole, eating's a joke, the symbiosis between pickle relish, say, and the triumphant predator scraping it across taste buds like a drug, nothing shall enslave, not food nor sleep, he shall offer no modicum of vulnerability: dehydration, defecation, asphyxiation *et al* belongs to the weak fallen upon earthly thrones of muck and ooze, he tightens titanium bolt into anus and strips the threads—indestructible internal concrete block which pathetically prays prays to him whose spindly legs crumple to piles of scrap, peace from him, king of hosts, judge of gods, superfluous sustenance, crutch of earth's incompetent, earth's idiots straining gruel through mustachios, fantasizing paradise, filthy kids stubbing toes and whining for fill, his last feast will be just that, river of concrete mixed with rocks topping his throat, quick setting concrete molded to gut, he will smash god in the gob and all dark night observe the sniveling mortals curled in sleep.

1477

I abandon the whole fucking enterprise, body weight, work, money, health insurance, home improvement, car maintenance, relationships, f. u. c. k. i. t. give me to bums, beggars, derelicts, down and outers, fuck creative writing, MFA shit, The New Fucking Yorker with its twits, The Agni Shit Hole Review so Boston University makes history puke up poetry like rat poison and that baby factory Iowa stamp molding bores like lug nuts, I' d rather eat my own gristle, my only fascination is my own goddam erection, my beautiful thick root stiff in hair, tusk curved, red purple alive in this pitiful world, squeezed by Mary's kegel tight pussy, or Janette's or Rosalie's, or by my own competent hand into a face towel beside cracked open porn, so fucking what that death strychnines mother, that bloody snake, so what failed Daddy who slammed his brains out for money shuffles in roach brown slippers, death his toothbrush, fuck them both up the butt with a broomstick, they napalmed each other like vietnam, blistered my sister and burned off their faces, the enterprise sucks, I pet my dick like a cat neck and gape toward the window, runway of littered desk, windowframe, screen, trees, rooftops, sky, the absurd futility behind angled walls, ok, if you want to fucking know if you really want to goddam fucking know the fucking pathetic truth about it all, it's all bloody lunatic, even squiring your little penis into a towel or cunt for a few silly oblivious seconds, in the middle of coming I say B. I. G. F. U. C. K.-I. N. G. D. E. A. L. S.O. G.O.D. D.A.M. W. H. A. T.,

God, sex, money, waistline, poetry, health insurance,
cleanliness, civility, new tires, it's all a load of crap,
as I said at the beginning of this exercise I'm sick of
the whole vapid desiccated idiotic dehumanizing enter-
prise, go about your primordial unconscious survival.

1476

I've got five chances left: God, food, love, kindness, death; God's the
simplest, pray and He'll pop up like a tube blister, a groin hernia,
God the simperer, the shamefaced cat skulking to the lap, "dear Fa-
ther," dribbles from lips and I'm absolved, lit; I ascend above God
and kick His gizzard for being ingratiating, bloated, nauseated, Chris-
tian gluttony, purging half-digested onion blossom and walnut
fudge, cells frozen, swollen, stretched, I stuff whom I hate with
what I loathe, twisted bread, chunk nut cookies, poppycock, step
requiring camel legs into the heaven of love I have none of, but
tender clay hot sand scorches, binger, bulimic, poseur, slender
fraud, bundt cake, milk shake, I crave and fill like mother craves
son; I step into love like a tub of butterscotch, it gooshes, baby
I blurt, sweetheart, buttercup, bunny of love, standing in pudd-
ing to my thighs feels amnesial, yet drugs make me lie, I'd nev-
er, rock-dependable, analyzed, feminist, the babe's given her-
self, then rages betray betray bastard and, yes, I squirm like the
murderer, I'm conscience but incorrigible, oh Ms. Right's push-
ing her Audi through sludge toward me, she'll arrive like Abis-
hag, Shelomith, Tabitha sweet on eglantine, an ocean blue pearl
machine with she inside like a coffee creme filling, I treasure
her, she's Love, the annihilating wall of it, crashing through
my mug the boulder of every crumb of it cleaned off the world,
love's incarnation cracking me between the selfsame entity's
thighs and biceps, crushing me to jelly; I strap on nursing
breasts, fill them, tilt his reeking head, he sucks, milk squirts,
traffic lurches by, sirens, clanging trucks, wretch and milk drib-
ble down his chin, filthy, matted, infected, perforated, pros-
thetic breasts pumped with life suckle this one mother's son
sick with substances, nearly dead in an improvised camp un-

der cold creekside trees, alone and terrified; on emaciated shiny knees before me death cowers, gutless, cowardly grovels, "return Mother, Daddy, and another, your choice, with whom you wish to commune—Vincent, Jeffers, Toscanini—my vault's treasureful—a fortune—take any three but spare me, I'll throw in personal immortality", spindly pathetic leg hairs, useless cock and balls, skeletal past tense reaper, I am plated invincibility, dying, death rides from me on a Galapagos land tortoise.

1475

She adores her tiny teeth, extra-white, tight in gums. Neck skin loose yet tendon undergirded, strong jaw-clench round darling tines of beef. Uplifted buxom tits. Broad hips. Milky Way of frecks, a light-skinned one. Speckles between cleavage. Two nape cakes. Domesticated eyes, innocent, amber brown whereas another's sparkle turquoise or various shades of gray. Hers is chestnut brown. Another's wrists impress, sinuous muscular wrists, but the Timex engulfs hers interlaced with veins. Virgin roves through her—the untainted waif—whistles while she soaks, marvels at my pecs, my "marvelous manliness", whereas cynical shrew crashes through Loretta, Mary Lou. She's delicate, not rank nor lascivious, not drilling hot piss into a snow hole, berry-pungent, etcetera, she's inexperienced at mounting males whereas Lori hikes her ass, opens from behind like a ravenous devil-bitch. She's never flipped to wag her rump nor shrieked bloody homicide. I could marry Lori or Bernadette, rough them up, bite or jam ridge-wristed Yvette's hand down my pants. My come repulses, she spits it on my tum, psychologically ill-conceived, orchidly. Innumerable women: experimental, straight-laced, brilliant, or dumb; globe-assed, pigeon-toed, posture perfect, or bowed; acrobatic, secretive, obsequious, or mean; battle scarred, obnoxious, trite, or incorruptibly pristine. I cannot make a life with anybody.

1460

I'm not your man, I lie on you and you come, you devour me like
vermicelli, weep, choke, above everyone your lips crave mine,
and I'm fond but not the one, you're in love with mr moribund
echoing addiction-splatter against padded thuds, I answer your
obsessive savoring with psychological conflict—brown mouse,
garage mouse skittering behind broom or stiffened rag when door
delivers serious human—you hound like chocolate lab amongst
the drunkards, slobberer to my indifference, historic old admirer,
I am spaceman tethered to mother ship, packed in tadpole mud,
on pumped-in sustenance, you thick skulled dog adore the lie
of me, 3-D, six feet tall, longboned, epiglottal, dear oh dear
not even ms smith's cherry pie can soothe this tear, me of the
american gynecological society and the academy of american
cads hauling in Bonita knuckle-over-fist from the jade green
sea, sweet baby jesus you blind your middle eye with me, fill it
to the socket chanting tuna gutturals and panting enumerations
while, crosslegged, from a chair I observe myself with you, heart
infinitesimal in intellectual blaze, I bring myself plate of pear
slices and bleu cheese topping biscuits to watch your weather-
vane toes blown ecstasy rigid, lower back locked on the acety-
lene torch, flank muscles shoving you to shuddering destitution.

1459

God and me, I punch, you fucker, the hollywood bloody nose;
god punches back, split ear; swing and miss; god lands one,
splits my eyebrow; I jab to the ribs, once twice, no damage;
God upper cuts, chin jams teeth jamming upper plate like a
stack of dishes, my neckbones rattle; I hug God for rest, then
nasty bastard knee him in the groin; God has neither balls
nor cunt, He bashes me in my plexus, windless the mat; I
unveil the magnum, blast Him in the face, dark wet hair;
God covers the wound with palms, it heals; heal me, I cry,
He cauliflowers my right ear knocking out bugles, then
cracks like a match stick with karate kick my left leg back-
folding it at the knee, my lower crab claw dangling, I crum-
ple; forgive me, I plead, I've sinned, I walk in the shadow;
God axes my spine with heel, crustacean fat, orange, bursts;
snapped I drag wet across floor, slug, jellied caterpillar;
God's whole foot bone knives right buttocks, withdraws,
stabs thrice, mangled blood flesh shell gristle ball; my work-
ing tongue: guile, adultery, malevolence, cruelty, treachery,
gross loveless insensitivity; God wads and crumples me
like a bag of dry spirals: skull, clavicle, pelvis, tibia, fib-
ula, ribs crack, thrust through, God's eyes glass marbles;
expiate, I manage, undo, leniency; mangled, slaughtered,
atrocious; God walks away, He wears cowboy boots, door
bangs; from my gut-pile crows and rats begin pulling strings.

1457

I have shorn and given to you, delilah, my hair, old squirrel, dog
carcass, my might, my potency like a dead cabbagehead, I loved
you like a spec the vacuuming suction, you pulled me back into
the cigarette, the paper unburnt, virginal, after blowing me out in
clouds, in rings, you silver gowned sophisticate, single malt, ice,
was it Barnard? Bryn Mawr? cultural anthropology? academia's
daiquiri cold, Alaskan moonchip planted inside neck skin, per-
manently, dear, human males rarely control sexual politics, yes,
I know, but still, kneecaps resemble monkey skulls, elbows the
cartilaginous nose, sampson hair tongue nodes I've shaved,
sprinkled over you, dish babe slut love desperate for, my shoul-
der blades shriveled doric pillars, chicken wings, your sandal's
big as cincinnati, brassiere cup guadalajara, ten thousand feet
above tree line mountaineer I stand in fanny pack like an idiot,
I've doffed toupee to your rhino, girly girl I'm broke on the
wheel, tatter windmill sails in low hung trees like medieval
battle aftermath, you egg beast, man predator, industrial milk-
er, in the barn fucked my lizard father, giggled, checked the
navy bean soup with a finger like an infant's fever, afterward,
nonchalant, insouciant, I unable to wring your neck, fingers bur-
nt candlewicks, I suppliant worship you, asian armored you,
my thrusting bony hips like a mechanized macabre skeleton
rattling themselves on massive sheets, dead desert cow, one'd
think it incontestable and necessary to my and clan dignity:
ditch the bitch for one of the innumerable available obedient
alternative chicks but hairless, prostrate I'm beaten, beaten.

1442

The sun will not rise on a man named Gordon dead by his hand,
there shall be no head blown off nor errant butcher knife,
creased cheeks will seek sun's rays—ravines of liquid gold—
Mr. Sun shall unearth no semen-coagulated towel beside a
pistol-torn heart nor will office machines grieve for their friend,
Gordon's fungoid toe shall crack again, his mangled finger-
nail disgust croaklessly, his voice shall wend into the bone, it
shall be a cornucopic day of drunk bananas and crosstorn
greens, erections sheepishly achieved, and dripped pee, let
there be grandiosity, the realtor-pin punched through lapel,
the Rockport wing tip shoe, motivational hair and a genuine
grin, it's toothpaste tube and electrical grid stringing lives
together like beads, god adores fingers and toes, the solar
flare shall not rise on Massman slain by enraged psycholo-
gy, he shall not snow upon field pieces of himself nor steep
in his own bathtub teabag, instead sugar bowl, cantaloupe
rind, dark yellow yolk, Scott paper roll, cat effluvia, chok-
ing marigolds, dirty windows smashing sunlight into toads,
we shall find G. at the real estate agency, crushed but con-
genial, greeting and exchanging dialogues with the unexploded.

1437

I break my own heart, I say I don't love you anymore, I say we are finished, I say your critical, I say I've lost patience, interest, passion, I say you are fat, I say I hate the wart on your shaft, I say I dislike your moles, I dislike your perfectionism, your pretentiousness, I say I'm sick of your victimization, I'm sick of your self-loathing, I'm sick of your sexual preoccupation, don't you understand, you think like a looser, a derelict, a whiner, I hate your hang dog posture and baggy clothes, I hate your carelessness which leads to breakage, lost keys, unpaid bills, disconnected utilities, it's not funny I say, it's a strategy of helplessness, of infantilism, you like to suck them in, then kill them, they come, you destroy, I'm exhausted by your negativity, your depression, your beautiful disease, the narcissist inside your feminine/intellectual/empathic persona, I break my own heart disavowing you, I take to bed, I heat the pillow, I review the litany of atrocities, your clamlike toes, your piston hips, your interminable thrust, the hopeful women sucking you in like a bathtub plug, stopping themselves with you, gullible idiots, I snap my heart like a peppermint stick decrying you, your corroding superiority, your invulnerability even to your children, your glued up tear ducts, quit my home, I'm disinterested, your meticulous microscopic measurements of vanity, your sloth, I say you are domestically useless blind to disrepair, corrosion, sloppiness, considerateness, you're a desultory, chaotic, unstoppable nonconformist insatiable toward happiness, defier begone, abstainer get lost, self-righteous czar take the hike, I tear my biggest muscle like silly putty you nipple-sucking, world-denouncing, father-hating, ego-smashing, self-destructive fucker. We are forthwith and forevermore uncoupled, goodbye.

1434

My ideal mate craves overlapping litters, she wants in-
finite babies, to birth a nation, a race to march through
her like soldiers through muck, lily roots, and rot, she
gods fertility, ovaries, fallopians, umbilici, womb, en-
ough years do not exist to deliver masters and slaves,
shopkeepers and kings, taxpayers and governments,
window washer with his lunatic squeegee cleaning the
eyes of idiots, SWM demands insatiable thighs spread
like carps' mouths sucking down thick lightning, clot-
ted hollandaise teeming with chives, no hair color pre-
ference nor economic stream just the insanity to deliv-
er offspring through canal, trachea, anus, and heels,
desperately, oceanic, unfathomable, bottomless, fuck
feminism, the whole goddam petrified substratum, S-
WM wants sorghum field, sugar cane field, soggy rice
acreage to propagate a race on a hot birthing bed near
buckets and rags, slop if it be, consider Harleys super-
fluous as hikes in dead leaves, I want dirty toes, stick-
y chlorophyll, phosphorescent gel like heavy wet lan-
terns produced through coarse hair, procreativity like
a potter's lathe placed in my trust, you: bony, fat,
thrust, gigantic, petite, blunt fingered, pulled glass,
salt manikin, laughs at anything, mustachioed or eye-
browless, pedigree irrelevant; me: lobster man, per-
ambulate clicking, bubble brine, arched calcium car-
bonate spine. broad, muscular, curving forehead into
your sex like a gyrating metal band, unrelenting, sed-
entary or athletic, blonde/blue, auburn/green, pedicure
irrelevant so long as the soles of your feet face heaven.

1433

Man distracts woman from self-deceit, without man she pretends the sanity of orderliness and spirituality, soft luminescent lunar creatures, tablets of the sky full of peaceful blue eggs and filigree thread, she accepts no earthquake from brutal male but wafts the blossom of universal peace through which men wage war like contrapuntal noise waving explosive phallic toys, extraneous sloppy unkempt men, domestically spastic against nurturing wholes; protect me from uncouth helpless aeternus beasts, those gluey tarbabies pulling out my peace, I denounce men's arrogant dictatorialism and their indiscriminate dicks, for example when Gwen's schnauzer died together with photos we wept and memorialized Mitzie's collar while emotionless fathers fired cold steel, drifted to work, where's the cloven heart in masculine flesh, let us pray for metamorphosis among the warrior class, we're covered in white brocaded silk, swollen perfect contained ocean unbroken inside underpants, rose surrounded, calla blessed, pale millionstar spilling its chest, organdy kissed, lavender, oregano, vanilla, cacao, sweet yellow nibs, beautifully veiled for the wedding with pure gristle.

1432

I stare at you, mercilessly, guiltlessly, burn you in my brain, my baked enamel core, with lust or revulsion, mathematical indifference, your coffee flat hot water, your pastry fried ether; your bones float in graphite gray under radiation scrutiny, you exhilarate, your nose, your hairstyle, the intersection of your Y, brittle wishbone; the bastards of civility, guarantors of privacy, decorum mongers in understated chic, fuck yourselves; I stare social graces into your soul like nails, I want to stroke you, I want to caress you, I want to slip on your glistening coat, I across the room, paperback, boutique coffee, nonthreatening thumbs, lousy poet, and longer strip you like butter leaf lettuce; fuck you, bastard, buzz off sicko but I stare on like a rapist; I am Jewish, educated, productive, masturbatory, insatiable, and self defeated, a wedge of cake sweeter than Belgium, I despise my father, think my mother a loveless whore; I stare at you like a wall, a featureless wall, melding your characteristics into flat latex, my cheap wooden table significant as a throne, six-thousand pounds of solid gold on marble floor, and you're an ordinary functionary fascinating in your ordinariness, unpresumptuous nondescript cupidinous psycho, I judge you from my table unsubtly after wacking off in the locked lavatory; there it is, my dears, a portfolio, a résumé, the genealogy of a mesmeric, festering, isolated weirdo, eyes stabbing into women two thick hairy wood-hard carrots.

1430

I eat my nervous system, lobster, scorpion, delicate skeleton and
go slowly mad fucking the girls and failing to work in Santa Fe
amidst adobe telephones ringing in rhyme, god love em,
I'm not joking, I've slipped out my spine and slipped it down my
irrepressible throat poisoning everyone like mad cow mignons kil-
ling the clientele at Marvin's Marbled Meats lit brothel red with
the chilled iceberg bar; I serve me on a platter like the Kensington
Club and a dozen babes ate their way into Presbyterian General,
throwing up, toes trembling like snakes shot with Daisy by dead
aim kids in rural Colorado; apple biting my heels black lights my
lips with radioactivity, they lit other lips like a head shop; I'm gra-
titivation-tainted, wild, lick them to orgasm, plow them to hell,
stroke them to heaven in a single gunpowder night, I low, I moo,
I bleat pure desire, I clean meat off nerve endings of my spine,
poison pukes my babies guts and dysentery their bowels in pub-
lic lavatories after partaking of me; hell, they too eat their spines;
we're helluva bouillabaisse, man and woman, a seafood chunk stew
of thrill and abuse; take Tandy, if she didn't suck a man right
under her husband's nose, and of course Joe vomited regenera-
ting toxins like an endless cargo train running up his throat, that's
the bloody truth, and Ginger, well, one can hardly speak it; so
there it is: the adenoidal animal, the yes-no animal troughing
at itself, walking warily between enemies in Niceville; I pick
clean the flounder bones, my central nervous system, and mess
up another baby in love's rocking cradle sending her to the hospi-
tal hotel lounge bathroom at midnight amidst slick *hors d'oeuvres*.

1428

Today he awoke with apples for eyeballs, bright red jonathans misshaping facial bones, two roasted pig heads on vertical platters, black swollen eyes lids cannot fold over, stems upward like rope fuses, big dappled bulging apples, visionless, pulpy, fresh but growing rotten and ripe for fruit flies, he would be a nest, and these things braided to the optic nerve like weird lanyards, love-transformations, hands into spatulas, knees into spuds, and orbital apples, she resembles the apple, rotund, globular, cupped, a round bumpy ball prying his sockets, they're all one apple—cores, hearts, achilles heels, mahogany seeds, appetites and rejections, coquetry and refusals, the sweetest little hooves—too many bushels, his face aches from gratitude; to a man a billion women flown together with compressive force into a mass resemble the apple crammed into his sockets at three AM, hard crisp ones squinching his face with powers of destruction, every molecule burgeoning with droplet of cider, he adores, he applies no discrimination, the disconnected molecules catch between his sockets rushing to his heart, this morning he awoke moaning with sweetness, big three-dimensional sweetness large as softballs, door knobs, hip replacement joints, he swayed, he knocked over candles, he stubbed right knee blind with significant brutalizing gorgeous orchard pieces.

1418

Help me say the word cunt without feeling dirty, land
the cut of faith above my eye like a fist, bleed Jesus fr-
om my pricked middle fingertip, blend into my frappe
extract of corporation, my head's covered in fur like a
clueless ducking cat, clashing garbage cans, fill me
with awe for geographical chasms annihilating with
soundlessness, you the savior inside my blank world,
my alchemist, give back my father to my taste that I
may suffer him re-palatable, thief, coward, gargler
with acid, mitpop the baseball powered by love in the
crabgrass beside the garage near the natal plum bush-
es, if you're transformational touch from my lips to
my mother unsnap the word "mother" like a Bill Hick-
ock shirt, oh boy, synagogue man, sanctuary soul,
eau de crucifix, pick the envy tick from my hair, per-
mit the syllables com-pa-ny to slip up my throat with-
out the blockage of stones, company, company, cor-
poration like a patriotic song, yank from the root out
my petrified soul the invaluable offering my lover's
name, that it may bloom in the thick of my tongue
like an orgiastic sycamore tree, I bastard, I son of a
bitch, transform self manufactured terrifying snakes
back into mother's sallow fat and impotent scarlet
nailed toes, good heavens but this is sick, free me
from preoccupation with, as if freshly potty trained,
my own huge adult bowel movements, frequency, dur-
ation, amount, consistency, my toddlerhood perpetu-
ated in my central parietal, wax-wick roar inherited
flame. Help me understand my own foreign language.

1414

Vulgar poet, disgusting egotist, porn purveyor, fixator
on genitals, mother/father loather, tawdry charlatan, mis-
ogynist, histrionic rager, life sucking bastard, downer,
cheap exhibitionist, public purger, adulterer, anorexic
nervosa, hateful specimen, controller, obsessive-com-
pulsive, sicko onanist of the public lavatories, murder-
er, vow breaker, man without solidity, professional suf-
ferer, helpless baby, user, loveless sex machine, mis-
representer of psychological wisdom, husband to poetry,
lover of nobody, seducer of darkness, sociopathic
bore, isolationist, emotional coward, uncompassionate
hypocrite, lazy fucker be gone with you, go away,
leave me alone, stop tormenting, pack and blow, take
your stanzas, take your computer, take your inky side-
kick, take your crate of manuscripts, take your ul-
cers and ugliness, take your psychodrama and disap-
pear, I adored my father, I enjoyed a decent childhood, I
treasure humankind, you suffocate, you suck life, you
dislike your offspring, you're inflexible, Mr. Narcissist,
hands like a pianist's, not worker's hands, not hands
capable of construction, sissy hands, precious useless
hands, tools, house, cedar, rock, build something, fix
something, pull earth over your hands worthless prick, I
midwifed pigs while you slathered Royal Lyme, we're
history, screw you, insatiate, misanthrope, malcontent,
plug-eared stonetongued brick-eyed fart, vanish in-
to your vaunted pleasuretecture of moisturized whores.

1411

He needed something huge, he lead his people into an ambush of starvation, they erected cravens, they fornicated like animals, they jacked off, they blasphemed like pirate-bastards under the cold moon, the moon spilling unspendable change, the goat-head moon, they gutted and ate dog seasoned with sand, they murdered, severed hands, magnetic god sucked manna to his hole like filings, the herd thirsted, curdled; he needed dumbfounding miraculousness, they galloped against sheer mountaincliffs crushing baby bones and preadolescents, he had spent his leadership capital and oozed "charlatan" through his pores, they would roll like an indifferent earthcrusher mashing him; a threadthin path trickled under his feet, cracking knee joints he ascended, clods, half buried sharkfin rocks, arid clicking wings, powderclouds bloomed around his feet, the flock appeared infinitesimally small like Seurat dots; something slammed into his brain, earth flattened his right facial hemisphere, a laser smashed, he felt his pubic bush burning, he had climbed extreme altitudes, it spoke, commanded at my flame do not look, it burned but did not consume, imperishible root, he yammered incoherences, electric monsters under eyelids, red death vaporizing at the last instant, breaking apart like concentric circles, crawled into his hands a book, two stone pages, his bony digits wrapped round it; they crawled below like insects, a yellow-blue flame reminiscent of kerosene intensified his dick-wick, the pages waved etched in magnificence; the throngs, the impeachment, the vengeful fools, the split-toed sandals, blood filled loins; his soles found soil, it had been olympian; they grew less blurry, the intestine draped golden calf, the sparkling wheels, the hammering celebrants, shot upright, deathly still, popping eyeballs; an irradiated possessed God-struck prophet saw all gaping at, descending the mountain, a blithering idiot embracing a wind-eaten headstone.

1410

The Jesus kite. A drooping string. A boy below. Two sticks perpendicular stretching Jesus. Stiff wind flies Him. He dips. He loops. The paper thwacks. Jesus shimmies. The boy sends messages. They slide up the string. On one he scribbles wishes. Jesus belly dances, gyrates Hips. Hi-Flier Kite Company of Nazareth, Galilee, printed His image on paper, plus instructions for assembly. A boulder lays in the field, an empty cave. An angel white as light. Scary white. The others flee. The boy however—his father taught courage—unspools twenty yards of string. A strong steady wind that day. Lays his craft face down in weeds, the back side bowed stick and knots like a stage scaffolding exposed, strides to twine, gathers it, runs away from kite and Jesus rises, vibrates, tugs past His tail, the boy grows small scampering in a field, eggbeater legs. Jesus speaks. "I indestructible." "I omnipotent." "I fear Dad." Furiously Jesus—crown, blood, gash, stigmata—tugs. The string snaps. The boy grows huge, heartburst, tears. Black world blurs. Low hanging clouds—a storm's foreshadow—swallows and sweeps Jesus somewhere over trees, beyond meadow, into impenetrable emptiness. A boy named Levi watches, spreads the word.

1399

"Come unto me and I will give you rest," for weari-
ness besets like overheated tar, shall rub your toes of
locust bits and clods, shall roll from cave of knees
filth, shall ply dirty gel from globes of buttocks, for
you carried through Saharas of love center beam of
the Word: gratitude, humility, compassion, ben-
evolence, exhausted, staff rotted, robe noon-bleached
and brutalized, I shall twist swabs into your ears and
lick shut eyelids like sweet vaginas selfless mes-
senger, bringer of tides; we will pour you skin of
wax and peel it off a norseman god, smite a fairy
wood nymph for you who craves fellatio and night-
ly penetration to bear you three sons and a female
glass cutter to cut you eyes of supernatural light that
bore into motive and disposition vaults surrounded
by bone for you spilled roe of hope, ambergris of
fascination, frankincense of levity, curry of indom-
itableness like the triumvirate of magi balled into
one captivating man, you taught me knight to bish-
op three, anti-self-cannibalism, moth collection for
lunatics, diaper magic among somnambulists, coin
crud. I shall clean your toenails with my teeth and tongue.

1381

Most amiable and loving beast which drew up Jesus
through straw like a milk shake, most amicable and
compassionate, artist handed, Harvard degree, Ital-
ian leather jacket, woman slayer and vanquisher of
rivals, I worship thee, knees down like a penitent,
knees varnished like skulls, your benevolence of
psalms, songs, and hymns, beautiful beast, claw-
pawed, incisored, scissor jaw, scythe of animals
and raker of kingdom, subduer of pharaohs and
blood maker of water, I eat you like saltines and
maketh of my heart wool habitat of swaddle for
your shoulders, back, curled into my firm embrace,
I bring you offerings—Nintendo, Transformers,
cream whipper, smasher of spud—lay upon altar
and slaughter Buzz Lightyear like a squealing dui-
ker for you preferment, Buzz's neck gushes like
a celery stick and I chant love love in warrior fash-
ion in my electronic paradise, and you, beast ma-
chine, who sucked up baby at thirty-three appear
cloudy faced, wet from fucking, dripping a bit
from a cottony beard female juice, yes appear
about my living room, exclusively, inhabit my
temple like a huge Eucharist, do you love me?
love me? I beseech, now that I've wrapped about
you like a skink, and you stutter, wwwell I've
watched you stststrugggle wwwwith girls and
fuck up ggggeennerally you little shit bbbbut I
fffind you palaaaatable nevertheless, love you,
ppprobbbably, with that vanished like a holocaust,

Kate Bush resumed, the digital minute flipped,
Mr. Frigidaire roared like a jet, and I after beast,
kind and ultraviolet, discover myself incandescent
lit among simple white tile surrounded by bucket,
comet, soft scrub, and brush kneeling at my john.

1380

Gof of the griffin; Gof of the Hemerkop; Gof of the fulmar, petrel and cahow; Gof of the Eastern Gorilla; Gof of the Pichi; Gof of the tamarin, jird, and boa; Gof of the paradoxical frog; Gof of the headstander, trahira, and cisco; Gof, Gof, Gof, humbler of Abraham, lionizer of Noah, breaker of Bulah into servitude, who maketh the penis a hypodermic of coke to the knobby clitoris; friend Gof, ogre Gof, misshappen Gof with medically botched face, concaven, splotchy, elephantine hairs; Gof of the spilling cornucopia and the microorganismic hockey puck; Gof red blow and pink flickers; black crumbly snouts and worried fur; Oh Gof I lay like a jelly fish before you my mental illness shaking opalescent in playful sun, squash me it begs under eucharist tongue, phylacteries, and crucifix; Gof I say, Gof the horrendous piercing heroin into baby flesh through glistening stingers, my hero among faint warriors in khaki and soil flags, fangless puffing adders worming in soil like lost patriots; Gof my lightning bug of Southern nights eliciting glee from short pants among honeysuckle; sweet dripping Gof pattering driveways and windowpanes in Corpus Christi swelling the scissor tails and and magnolia bees; my vengeful, forgiving, perfectionistic Gof the rabbinical Nazareth set in tough roots and needle flowers, lizards and horned axioms; I produce you into towels, wipe you off tip quivering like cranberries in shivering; some in Benedictine celibacy, some in nonsecular mediocrity, some in heartplunge sacrifice, some in Samaritanism, some in pablum applesauce, some pituitary wack-rage; Gof, I shaved off slice of parents, cleaned off wedge of mate, peeled skinful sock down to red disease, crooked thumbs in and unrolled underwear over unguent smell, slid into hot Dove water and rubbed rubbed my sin and rank iniquities and terry; I stand pink, scrubbed naked among lunatic tiles like a pistil pale white privates and upperarms for you to pop off like a sniper or bless like the parkinsonian pope, Gof my absentee amputation or doxology who maketh from the mulchmush pippistrelle, vicuna, mangabey, houbara bustard, little chachalaca, kinkajou, natal duiker, by-the wind-sailor . . .

1379

Huey, Dewey, and Louie bring home three whores for dinner.
Huey gets spanked and blown, Dewey's a blind patient at the
doctor's, Louie does it dog style on the sheepskin throw, three
women contain duck come like mechanically filled mustard
jars. How they worship zooming tits, purchased lips, the soft
slot machine of the naked woman. A stogie turns Huey green
poor mallard, night's growing sour, the promise of vomit,
frankly diarrhea's looming in guts of three like bruisy storms,
but hell we're men aren't we? gimme a Pabst, and red be-
tween the orange webs sucks off his purple cock, and even-
ing drags, dies, the females split, the males blacked out, ash
trays, tumbler rings, mixer packets, missed chunks, Donald
and Daisy anticipating an after the movie tumble pissed at
the profligate nephews, sailor suits and menstrual blood. Don-
ald to Daisy: God dammit! Daisy to Donald: fuck! Donald
to Daisy: Look at this shit. Daisy to Donald: Idiots. Dish-
washer filled, blender upright, the boys covered in blankets
where they lay, Daisy fucked Donald hell for leather till
both sets of genitals failed with satiation, Donald stunned
with love, penis a limp sore biceps, Daisy drunk with semen,
inside out like a flaccid flower, hiving for conception, both
fired and blown apart, hinged at the knees. Oh Donald, Oh
Daisy, Oh Huey, Dewey, and Louie, swaddled, lifted, and
held by God, suckled on heaven's nipple, do not sob the flesh-
y mess of eggs and lust, sperm and hurt, the slimy floor of
booze, musk, and promises; sleep, safekeep, angels angels angels.

1378

Dear and venerable King of rodents roaches and duikers
humbly I beseech—your criminal sinner, your unmention-
able execrable, dick wielder, homicidal fantasizer, wom-
an meat grinder—on skullcap knees bloody with grovel
I cower to Your Omnipotence like a thunderclapped bow-
ser, dear Father to whom mountains are granules, I slice
an eyelid and offer You blood, I slice my urethra and
peel my penis walls along the straight razor's edge for one
absolution-drop from Your immeasurable head, my sympa-
thetic host, I feed live cottonmouth down the throat for
an inch's forgiveness under Your fabulous dome, find
me in synapses and make of me a whore's come buck-
et, vengeful and revered almighty Executioner whom
I fear like insomnia, crook Your finger up my ass and
blow me apart like a nuclear device for I fashioned of
receptive flesh stone, stood before my baby encased in
granite palms facing up as if inside a door, but if it's
exoneration heap upon me multiple clitori, Corvette,
and Bugatti; leather riding pants, one Panerai, one Ro-
ger Dubois; unbow my legs into Cooper stride, de-ros-
aceate my cauliflower bulb into Lee Van Cleef, Kirk-
land "Sparticus" Douglas such that applause explodes
under dome of carved winged horses and blossoming
whales, mint me—fornicator, alcoholic of flesh—blem-
ishless, razor-shaved acquittal or decapitate my fin-
gers then hang me by the heels over sponges of dirt
for I am big air beyond tribunal or jumping to ham-
mer blows just above the hips, You skewer pig through
anus out snout, roast it over pit, ambiguity's not Your
forte, nor this cabinet of knives insists, must be it mine.

1377

Exploded charred heart like a burnt bird, put-
rid, crispy, prehistoric turd in curved sabers,
mama cupped his eyes fearing the thing suck-
ing junior down to diabolical coven caves thick
with crows and sacrifice, the ominous black
love machine wicked out, spat as cat hairball,
nuked feathery ash in archaeological hell, and
on comes this doofus in goatskin sandals, gaunt
hollow-eyed huckster, desert blown abstraction
like something from Goya, thunderstruck with
schizophrenia, twisted warped obscene escap-
ee from Galilee, all knees and metatarsals, but
recommended by lepers as a gifted physician—
old roasted bird, electrocuted, quasi-fossilized
aforementioned turd scraped and blew itself to
curb, naked, desolately visible, striving to not
resemble ox shit sticks out its dehydrated tongue
like worm from clod, and this unseemly maes-
tro risking contamination, like a compulsive per-
former of ceremonials, lays on hand, glares know-
ingly (dramatic megalomaniac, crack addict, third
trimester whoreson abortion), fried turkeybuzzard
like a Looney Tunes maroon on reassuring rumor
curves upward toward his palm: illumination, shoot-
ing rays, orchestral cymbals, hails down plopping
before the Christian scripture, ground like preg-
nant centrum rumbles, mountains quake, water
veins the cremated puff, bathes its passageways
such that poor broasted idiot, faith infused, be-

lieves like his pancreatic neighbor and Laz on
the east bank, it shall miraculously be to func-
tioning heart restored, it salivated for new erect-
tions, seductions à la bourguignon, a bachelor pad
beneath mountain peaks cloud shrouded and fal-
con swept, but neither upon its tongue flooded cata-
clysm's life blood nor into muscle pump like a
lubricating tun, the blistered spent devastated chunk
receives zero, Son's a dud, coughs incineration-ash
from its ventricle bag as the calves, heels, and staff
hobble away like an ass across glowing Palestinian sand.

1375

I give myself an award. Here, I say, is an award and pin a hyena's balls to my chest. They are neither roasted, boiled, nor baked but hang hairily sagging my shirt pocket, raw: Dissolution III, bankruptcy, and an indissoluble addiction to woman. I wear my red genitals like water balloons. The National Academy of Lunatics presents me with a castrated animal longing for his genitals, eyes like buckets of rusty water, and I deliver my acceptance speech, "I'm overjoyed, I'm thunderstruck, this above everything was effort collaborative, I wouldn't be gloriously standing before you without my director Mother Seductress, my producer Daddy Implacable, my supporting actor Unpluggable Vortex, and of course my cinematographer Ostentatious Animosity in Ascot and Leisure Lunacy Accented in Mango Gold. I kiss the crowd and exit, my two jewels swinging like breasts. With these leathery sperm factories whom shall I now trap? Norma? Nancy? Tourmaline? Kimberly? The stupidity of romantic preferences, men fantasizing in tub on the Atlantic, jacking off tree trunk thick cocks, drowning in come. And I with my contemporaneous medal round the corner to McDonald's, stride to counter, the usual, chest jutting like a General, like a power snatcher's granite pecs, prepared for innuendo and insinuation, umbrage and wiggle-waggle, W.W. id est the Fourth, breaker, biochemical, thermonuclear, which is nothing but acidophilous, squirmers teeming in atropined eyes, from inside their quivering water drop round which they whirl the starry host, bacilli, open mouths soundlessly screaming.

1373

Smeared across God's face excrement, beet pink, seed gray, potato smooth, fished it from my john and scrawled unnamable antiquities in the primeval vein—diarrheic sounds, magmatic utter—defiled, degraded Omnipotent One, improvements on transparent invisibility, Dear Big, I shit your hair with hot dinner, I the lover and benefactor of women, I the pacifist; I push into my log as impressing into clay the origin of East Wind His alcoholic nose, seal His canons like two canning jars and skip to my lou my darling for piss I scoop with two hands and open on His chest, diluted, pinkish too from those copious beets last night chewed in pintos and meat, my psyche's prize chili, God the exposed, the banished, the disgraced, dump streaked wandering excommunicant, and fuck this metaphorical poeticism, narcissism dismantled three marriages of the journeyman variety filled with casserole dishes and Paula Zahn, cardamom and Columbia Pictures, the functional, dependable kiss-by-peck impregnability by which boards on ledgers are laid level, insatiability destroyed this like a scaled fish, and all that crap fifty-three years couldn't erase, a vicious seductress mother trailing tampax string from her thick black wedge fondling my genitals with Revlon nails, Daddy Adjutant of the broom and impregnated sawdust set spewing commands across his concrete warehouse stacked with Mars Bars and Lorillard, and dunking my head into the employee john flushing like a bomb, Lord love his spit, and the two powerful engines of kill awaking anew to slaughter each other by the dunk of the sun, their babies rocking in freezers of their beds, their later lives over-lathed into grotesque cedar sticks, and so I defile the King who is I with

my own lousy shit at the asylum of ache with a jumbo white
chalk like the mentally disturbed child, until He is covered,
my raw quartered meat—ribs, shoulders, spine—in brown under-
side of which perfectionism, self-pity, and neediness collide.

1344

Verbal directions are horrid: "left at the traffic light across from Burger King, which is Pearl Nix Boulevard, no Parkway, but don't turn on Ashford which is easy because there's a McDonald's, make sure it's Burger King, not McDonald's; then left on John Murrow, there's a huge bank catacorner, Wachovia, I think, and a Target, no Shopko, isn't it Shopko, Sweetie? on the left corner near the Long John Silvers; then straight for about one-two-three-four, about six blocks, then left at McKenzie, no, not Mackenzie, Mc . . . Mc . . . McKendrick, McKendrick, at a Blockbuster, there's a Radio Shack, too, then you'll go past an office supply store, a group of single storey tan brick edifices, you're heading away from town, southwest, no east, southeast, you'll see a bunch of ramshackle commercial structures, a blueprinters, a roofers, a plumber, an Enterprise Car Rental, Borg Engineers is out there—I've used them—I think you'll see on your right a Dominos or a Papa John, one of those, just keep going straight till you get to an old town residential district and ultimately Number 801, the streets start being numbered, it's easy, sequentially, First, Second, Third, and so on, go to Eighth and you're there, I think it's on the right side of the street, but no matter, you'll find it." Horrid, even if one transliterates to paper, scrawls a map, reiterates. Horrid if the cargo's a twenty-one year old boy. Horrid if the boy's your son, concave, possessionless, billowing. Horrid if he's feigning in the back seat competence, nonchalance, insouciance. Horrid if domestic altercation and dissolution's ax-blow clove him to his coccyx. Horrid if it clove the chicken part of his song to the ball joint. Horrid if you, the driver, abandoned him at nine Horrid if his step-Dad, no matter how sweet, rides shotgun jabbering about Iran. Horrid if convection waves blur pavement. Horrid, the town harbors a maximum security prison. Horrid, the McDonald's, the Burger King, the KFC, the Taco Bell, the Chick-fil-A, the Subway, the Papa Johns, the Wendy's Old Fashioned, the TGIF, the Wok and Roll. Horrid, balloons strung to used cars. Horrid the boy's undeniable sociopathololgy and momentary after-binge humility. Horrid the menagerie of obese, impoverished, uneducated, nicotine-addicted, teen belly swollen, fundamentalist, Dixie confederate, polyester green suited citizenship. Horrid goose shit on the windshield. Horrid Dad's brokenheartedness and pseudo psychoanalysis. Horrid the Nissan ripping through Chickapin, Ogeechee, Possomhaw, Pignot. Horrid fertilization, multiplication, placenta water, rubbery organism devouring resources, demonstrating rage. Horrid exhausting fatalistic unsnappable predictability of slammed integrity and deterioration. Horrid needle-pricked father's son snapping Marlboro filtereds off his lips, flicking butts, cognitively pacing like a manic animal. Horrid mortal instructions through human municipalities named Sawtell, Quigley, McNaughton, Finn; pinging tappets, quavering camshafts, engine ooze, gear slime, lube and grease, squeezing gunk through heavy steel teeth, asphalt enzymes disfiguring tread, biologies occupying perambulators of their ingenious devisement. Horrid, *The Way Up*, three ultra-rudimentary syllables designating a residential adult addiction recovery facility awaiting my precivilized male genetic descendent at twine's end.

1333

Behind every holocaust lies a broken love affair, platelets bulldozed, corpuscles cremated, cortexes bulletholed, rifle-butted, tongues licking pavement stones, medically experimented testicles; shattered fascist spitting before multitudes, rejected; mate thigh-clamped, garlicky, obese uncouth, vindictive; perpetrator of genocides bangless save the fist, throwless but in toilets, jism springing into meatless air; eats himself; bones gassed, dying; eyes kicked out; concussion eardrums; glottis ripped out like fish throat; the vermin exterminated to nakedness, burning essence, exposed nerve chord scraped by cold air; by columns and communities the unclean fall—strong spared for digging—methodically, spasmodically, mob-mentally, lone psycho pathologically gigging, charring, bludgeoning, hanging after mock comical courts, an efficient machine, each clench-jaw turn of hamburger crank a wife curse, bitch!, idiot! cunt! whore!, ground human pie tubes forth like shepherd doo; country clogged, state stained, glory tarnished like sad molar, historically ripe, the filthy had to go like floss and plaque. Cut glass Baccarat hurled by nails lacquered "aorta red," totalitarian doubles over, orders his cranial oven stoked for cyanide and the feeding in of women, carrots plunged in high-pulp juicer; low white cell count, ulcerated lining—even demagogues, divorce-self-devouring, snap like piano wire, opening a slack eternity between chords; everything worth extirpating dead, the Propaganda and Public Education Minister pheasant hunting, the Chancellery of State lido combing, the Homeland Defense Czar fucking, the Personal Secretary motortouring Shangri-la, the Interior Minister disgorging aquavit, and the venerable lieutenants centrifuged into wealth, the raging butcher, stripped of will, pushes his final ligament regiment into the sea.

1327

Chastisement as prayer: Comforel under head, fist under Comforel,
tee shirt nakedness, "Dear Fuckface, Cunt, Buttswirl, Uranus: a land-
mine near Kabul hasn't fulfilled, lays fallow in hunger, dispatch it a
boy, shrapnel wedge penis, foreleg by thread, Cuisinart head, but
command him live fifty-four years, bitter, enraged, childless, sad;
Dear BastardShit, burst 'genocide' on lips like toad throat, rip
Kurds into scorpion coral snake worm bait, shove muzzles up fe-
males' ass, blast, double medals for pregnant; Dear Betrayal, Glock
husband Horrid, he thirst's a kill, blood the chaise like lacquer,
projectile through wife's head, gracias, Great;" knees drawn
like sitter, balls flopped back thigh, stuck little, soundless but
wife's twitter, Hunter Douglas blackout coal ("Jasmine Green'),
"Dear Peewit, need I enumerate to Omniscience It's own mal-
adroitness? Meta-awareness, You. I'm minuscule on Quallofil.
Yet, despise you, naughty to Judaism, I must for Your card-
iac surgical botch-job, chest hemorrhaging, bloody urine, trach-
ea squeezing respirator, patient critical, and You with mask and
clipboard informing the family; Frankincense, Myrrh, sweet Amber-
gris, I honor You Himalayas, Mediterranean, The Pillars of
Creation, Cardiff-by-Sea, The Mariana Trench, Nine Banded
Armadillo, Vampire Squid—all geophysiological exquisite and
revivifying—but incomprehensible backdrops each to robotic
malfunction in domains of egotism, optimism, truthfulness,
liberty, and intimate relationships, so 'gather ye corpses as ye
may' in paradisal Haiti, dogtails wigwagging, bananaquits
chitchattering, dirty beige uniforms; dear Merciful Thou, on
fluffpuff I adjure—thorny legs, baby pate, elbows plucked—
surrender, emerge, amnesty Your hostages, disperse Your
Earth or cloudy disguise, walk out full-featured relinquishing
wand like Easter ribbon, though You may in my pulp indwell,
that creatures may comprehend around whose hand—savage,
embattled, heartbroken, soulless, and inauthentic—they spin."

1323

Head burst on fire when he removed hood, how could any head take it without igniting? World history is splattered bladder of red paint on wall. Head burst into ball, each flametip an eye, each eye a wagon. Look in craw. Carnage atop carnage. Old Thomas goes a'courtin with Lorna on lips and sulphur in gut, ice sheet union slides over confederacy, burlap of maize and ground Apache bone, kidnaped Noah's Franklin's semen balloon, dead, shallowed. Vision lights fuse, gunpowder smell, eight cranial plates. Love, etc.; a brilliant fiction; nuthatches et al; San Louis Obispo; Musée des Beaux Arts; Sunday with Hoover; Kali's karate lesson; waffle rocky road cone; Killy's cold Zermatt; Dubey & Schaldenbrand; strolling solar Auschwitz, arms clasped under cauliflower boughs; ricing Mai-Lai; Glad preceding Al down Slip and Slide on Super 8 film; Lion's Club Black minstrel show; popped corn in Kosovo; Captain Marvel slaughtering aqua people, Saturday afternoon at Bijou; moon eyed in Palestine; the Greater Westminster Dog Show and Pet Exhibition (Spice Girl BOS Winner); Spanky and Our Gang; Swan Boats of Commons; entertainment Rushmore paper place mats; bacon cheese cooled by double straw malt, Jerseyville, Illinois; fishing buddies-skipjack snapshot, East Timor; antiquing in Willamette; South African surfboard riding; and, knee on buckled buck outside Bozeman, stocks soaring, Stacy plastering Harvard, revitalizing awaiting extramarital affair: computer chip planted in brain, open eyes shut, plasma screen, Halcyon days! hot dog!, head lead-encased automatonishly, hooded impenetrably by sleepless metroplex, transfixed applauding-crying-and-laughing-induced audience, save intuitive fish-smelling revolutionaries who regardless Time/Life, Baskin Robbins, Dain Rauscher, Boston Chicken, ignorant of consequences, wrench off full metal jackets flipping upside-down on virgin shocked walls bloody sabbaths, shoe mountains, stump babies, shrapnel-lodged Kampuchean penises, ammunition hitting education like cloud of locusts, six pointed crematorium, prolific crop-fields fertilized by carbonaceous human remains, satanists melting through rising flame, bathed cuticle-removed powdered statesmen, beach sand packing soldier openings, black package gushing red blood onto white sheet, the dead shoveling trench-gashes, worshiped compassionate demagoguery, liposuctioned red undesirables, nailed resulting abomination of region Xq28, all ghosts, corpses, specters, shades, twisted, contorted, writhing, re-tortured before eyes as if scrawled on cardboard by schizophrenic girlchild institutionalized for self-injurious episodes and brain stem psychosis, thereby detonating their heads like mid-launch bibles with revelatory luminosity.

1320

Wind-ripped rain blows sideways off a concrete edifice, a gray-white blur of hurricane velocity off the ruled edge, human face into the gale flattens featureless made of sand, sheets stream off appendages in the shape of appendages, iron hammer strikes ten, twelve, fifteen, twenty-four, howling tsunami, Bonneville Bugatti, flesh withstands not the geology, Samuel bones, Majesty bones, Tenacity bones, shirt sail-billowing, pantlegs slapping, a man, arms outstretched impresses a cross in the onrushing clay of air, from peak of thighs a woman drops a child onto street before tumbling backward like a weed, everything flies on gut strings tethered tight, the wacking paper kites of cow, goat, rooster, peafowl, hound, javelina, and human; a jowl skin grain detaches, soars upward like debris, the whole jowl follows like a message, naked skull in the stiffness; visit the physician—serums, inoculations, vaccines—concretize resistance against the tropical named Gretta, Mercy, Eugene; aerobicize the physical on belts, chains; traumatize muscularity with stacked dead plates; hatchet halves wind, tissue decomposes before it; a blizzard whistles off First Federal Consolidated, sweeps down alleyways, and the leaning into, jutted forward, defiant, stalwart shudders round a crumbling drummer.//Broken windows crack world only when gazed through, diagonal split fractures no crow flight nor mountain thrust, pure as urine; after heating on naked coils and dropping into ice water, I re-inserted into its socket my eye ball shattered like a kid's glass marble throwing fractioned image onto wall: unforgivingness, rivalry, victimization flipped, hurled upon the cave, ingrained where clean streamlined object smoothly exists unsevered by division of lens. I have always loved you.

1317

Sander takes off skin and grains of skull, guided by carpenter passes again, again, head into curvaceous ball, red-wet shoulder-plumes, blue bone; artist-woodworker with number 50 grit orbits off total epidermis, refines consecutively with grits 80, 120, 320, then four ought steel wool, sculpting figure into smooth, faceless, fleshless bone, eyes-nose-mouth-groin holes rounded like stone, atlases, scapulas, occipital, astragalus, humerus and ulna, navicular and cuboid, the cuneiform complex contorted, bent upon themselves, twisted to artist's taste, polished like steel; convex of kneecap cradles cranium, left leg pretzled behind clavicle, ribs cracked and soldered to resemble tusks, teeth sharpened, blunted, extracted, drilled into faceted jewels; stainless rods up coccyx form a stand; the fragile confection-de-calcium bubble-wrapped, placed amidst a truckload of compatriots, and shipped to warehouse-metropolis to amuse tourists, mendicants, dignitaries, and capitalists. Hunger grinds people into artifacts and labor satiates hunger: steampressers, pipefitters, bricklayers, glass molders, iron workers, signalmen, boilermakers, longshoremen, heat & frost insulators, business entrepreneurs self-ass-kicked sopping yolks with toast, aerospace engineers, the brimming multitude of middlepeople under the scraping granules; the instant before EST voltage cauterized his brain Daddy muttered the insensibles: failure, ruined, broken, inventory, amortization, leg flying behind neck, hands folding backward, elbow stabbing spine as he bit hard; Bubba's upside down face between ankles staring behind as pharmacist plies him with anti-bankruptcy Amoxapine; Birdie's children' relentless duodenums growling a ballad tie her thighs into two

half hitches and split her sternum like cordwood to be
carted to megalopolis's Museum of Modern Antiquity; heart
scraped from ribs, brain vacuumed out, vulva smeared,
testicles ground, long muscles mangled and rolled, arteries
splat, intestines, kidneys, spleen ripsawn, nerve branchia
schismed, interstitial tissue—fibrils, laminae, gelatin, chords—
gnawed, gore-flown; shapers, sculptors, blasters, finishers.

1316

Against my will, I rip down zipper, shove porno before face, grow tumescent, and rape myself. Rapist fist-squeezes, tears undercircumcision tissue, violences orgasm into toilet, and bangs away like a striking hawk leaving me on carpet weeping. Crisis response team, rape squad, description (shot sharded glances in mirror), unrpedictable, unexpected, brutal, Caucasian, fled into the night of self, vast, anonymous like a whiptail; rage, not sex; revenge against distant abusers; howl in heart; injustice gnawing cerebral wires; I've not confessed—shame—he's hit before, cracked open hard core and beat incessantly ripping out my stuffing and fled like a murderer into my soul, slaked on subjugation and spermatozoa. I can take victimization by his hunger no more, the horror, the shock, the degradation amidst a beautiful world, his closet appearance irrepressibly, he's always within dead bold perimeters, his shoe-toes replicating mine and the gutturals wrenched out his throat iterate details he could not know; Karen's tampax, Sheila's lubrication, the exquisite blood orange and yellow pipefish, the unexpurgated yank through caverns of emptiness, cravings of Joyce, weird tectonic schisms in the earthplates of stability; my superinformed assailant confusing me with identification; smashing my dick between fist with jackhammer-aching arm, he hallucinatorily grunted, "fucker, you are me," then incomprehensibly vaporized the instant my come blew me off its string; pride terrorizes—I've slaved, I confess, for years, homosexually, painfully, grievingly, plumbing swallowing my esteem; the tidal sucks off a devastation-home. No more: hazel; six feet; gray wreath-tonsure; straight teeth; cupcake mole, left shoulder; moustache; olive; one-ninety; deceptively soft spoken; black bush; left lobe crease; fiftyish; big fingers. Grab handful of flesh, wrap fist, rip him through sewer grate to light, to justice, imposter, fake socialite, slime-liar, hit/run impresario, abominator of stainlessness and gorgeous stacks, chickadee household blackguard bastard.

1315

Religion breaks out like a cholera epidemic: singing, killing, filled sanctuaries, phylacteries, prayer shawls, crawling censers; God blasts out hearts like Batman; Billy kneels bedside; Shelly begs forgiveness; Mahatma, spirit struck, refuses further masturbation; believer-tides sweep Jerusalem, Fatmas hack mainframes, logon passwords like lambblood, blasphemy, 2coming; the revolution in psyche shoes; mama pierces babyears and foreskins fly like potato peels; necklace of automatic hangs off boy, but biggest believer wields phantom imbued with Word; soldier of protesting hoard, cutaneous, subcutaneous, meaty cells, and bone, busy terminal and seed factory, an organismic world to wall-splatter or pearl; columnar infinity. Innocents inhale airborne spirillum, illuminate, cry, vision of two floating sticks, bloody moon, empathy beyond containment, some pour into Africa contagion, complete with nail guns and ingenuity; others head for urbaniforousness, arrow into city, spread like silverfish; abortionists die and fetuses kick like Carnegie's Rockettes; fields covered in monolithic species: bluebonnets, Susans, chamomile: militarized Christianity; God blows corpuscles into our blood and we whirl, gather, refuse, knit impenetrable as The Rock. Infidels inject an antidote, a black mirthless bacilli lead-heavy casting them into a pod of immunity which vacuums zygotes and boils scripture into consume-literature, flaunt Amalfi and ball each other's mates, sulphurous impunity; Patrick and Dana camcorde Ginger grinding Constantine, then unpeel the X and exit oppositely flipping off the apocalypse. Conglomerates begin the games, blocks collide against blocks which edge-chip—a sea of needles—then, eaten, crumble, and finally granulate into confused mayhemic scrambling; lance pierces noble heart of horse, dogs lick, gulls outpeck glittering eyefleck; the games, the games, the salmon-emerald rules spawning resurrectable winners and losers flambé, coliseum faction-crackling, wave felling millions. Heavy bone vault cannot control its three pound grey matter pushing through goofy grotesquerie of Buddhas, turtles, yapping foliage, stags, floods, fireflies, fish, cosmic eggs, monkeys, goldeneye ducks, kidney beans, bananas, mole, Papantonakis, horsemen, and eye-rimmed wheels, like mallet and frying pan springing out Daffy; cranium explodes, populations expire of diarrhea, anuria, acidosis, and shock—too much God. Mother outpushes neonate finger-shooting lightrays, awe-striking the infidels, magnetizing the malevolent, and motile by means of a polar flagella.

1311

Dear and most of all venerable mother—death for you I fear is close, I heard you cough and know you blacked at Charlie's funeral, you slur words, and make intuitive macabre jokes; body knows what brain—feeble overrated meatloaf—does not; your bristly beard betrays another world; your children circle you like sharks; dear and most sacrificial Joan, rot becomes you like Marshall Fields; blood drop fingernails hard as dice; we could sink you in your Coup DeVille; fingers depress grieving eyes into lugubrious firework displays, out blows the back of head when I meditate upon my birth canal dead; escaped to Alaska, I've recircled to the virtual bed, you stink of gingivitis and cardiac malfunction, sour external organ breath, salamanders between toes; I was your beaux amidst three failures, I killed them each, one by bludgeon, one by pills, one by gas for you for you, fertility queen, symbolic pederast; now you're toast, anyway toasting between filaments of fire and I'm frozen like a mastodon in ice enveloping a bubble of disbelief-breath. I retract my malevolence; I've fantasized wiry black nests for years, Frankensteinian coarse hair and orgasm red gelatins along my shaft like suction eels pulsing strings of my balls in air; you the standard by which rivals fall stung by overhead scorpion tail; I love you, fusion and fission weld us to Siam, one lower colon, one number five cervical disk, genitals like Janus faces rotated on coccyx stick, inferno melded buttocks back to back, we are our individuality; I whiff that death has entered our room, some reeking insatiable masturbatory Rhesus squatting on the Mohawk and eating brownish mash; I withdraw former vituperations, by the tail dangle them wriggling before eating, gag on old words. Mama, tenderheart, CreamofWheat, the alphabet pinwheel spins;

He's inslipped boudoir—stabbing, vomiting, subatomic rage,
the inexplicable indentation of peace—surgeons of separation,
near theater, with spider-precise fingers await with tray con-
firmation that, like a paste, peeling off my side, you are, slain.

1309

The borders melted: borders that dammed all figures from bursting, table, window, coffee mug, man; all slammed together like paint; Joey puddled, laked; Hamilton's eggshell cracked, spread, mitosis of atoms; Franklin's eyes running decried his fingers stretching; Chloe pulled off her face; had not President decomposed, President would have declared national emergency; tires of scrambling F-16s interpenetrated tarmac like marshmallow into caramel; some hybrid undocumented goo did all default to: pith, lead, CO2, polyurethane, frog guts; mountains rushed down themselves and sharks inked up like clouds; the child-jammed black-crayon boundaries of bird, basketball, boat, building; the earth a sticky ball of indiscriminate copulation; atoms of the baritone's larynx mouthless as sand; well, here's an apocalypse: hate's armless spitless fizzless micro-organismic particles flowing against the hated like diarrhea, disgust's granulation grinding across its husband like an irony, coupled lovers rushing through and ungraspably past each other—the great ha-ha; debris indistinguishable from fries; who shall rescue?; Robert Cornthwaite? Takashi Shimura? Kevin McCarthy? Raymond Burr? Mighty Mouse? The ever triumphant offended God's henchmen who prevented the mauling of a neonate including the irreparably damaging bashing of its head by its mother's plastered freshly-fired boyfriend, not the biological father, too late. Science pronounces the reversion of matter to the preternatural state predicament-saturated without a predetermined febrifuge; viral? bacterial? parapsychological? Revelatory execution? And it came to fact that cesspool rose to steepledom, serotonin reuptake inhibited snake to bishop's blood, trichinosis spirillum to the thiabendazole compound; and all was oceanic, featureless, homogenized, latex-esque, and monotonously level.

1303

Crows scrape through my ducts, flight from eyes, dry, dust-
y, desiccated crows; I deliver tears like humans' babes, max-
imally one/year, Demerol, saddle block, clip-the-slit episio-
tomically, suckle; I'm crammed block-concrete. Little inter-
course with poignancy conceives a crow; little copulation
with gratitude fibrillates my egg; I'm bulwark-fertility; orange
beaks, black claws membrane rip; I support bridges with
insensitivity; can you gaze unemotionally upon psychotic
protoplasm, arterial intervention, species extinction; at Mo-
ther's graveside I froze mold-solid; ape-chested, iron
hefter, shiny palmed creature who loathes liquid, wetness,
and squishy minds; your tears are failure of appropriate
pride, mine are iron-feathered crows rarely liberated
lacerating mucous lined jellies; you weeping men soft as
April sod, I am boot-stubbing granite wedged in ground
like a molar; how it feels to cry: like pushing out binded
fecal material petrified with cheese, dough, and secrets,
sharp-edged, painful and then the crow pecking my food-
pupils. Therefore six inch thick reinforced internal walls
on honeymoon, in mainspring's tick, against offspring's
jaw, after grace's fall; zip; imperviousness of the upper
lip observing heartflaw, reverse megalomania, legsuck
in planet's hip; I learned quick and now not even charg-
ing bull scabbards or pate foie gras, hammered, events
implicating chordates, central nervous systems, or the
beneficiaries of overlapping litters disintegrates; post-
age stamps ox me solid, M. Monroe's subway freezes,
Giulietta Masina trowels face-blockages, and M. Falcon-
etti, that melted crystal chalice, solders my ears; ram-

med to ground by fifty-foot long stick, fixed, ice-sheet-
ed in purgatorial winter, uppermost limbs clacking in
wind, or stiff as frozen carrots; incapacity's resignation:
from the promontory of my cheek, an echoing cackle.

1301

Step outside your body sucking a hole in the air and make it get divorced, debased, or sick; lunatic, it does not feel, permitting you—the authentic self—to turn away, a stranger; the shill love-conflagrates lighting the dark with flame, acheless, providing combustions of air, he's a sick fucker anyway, it's not you burning but some depthless maniac; you possess rectitude, do not deserve to curl, let it lie beside her pathology while you, racing, orchestrate, accomplish, deposit, virtually innocent; split, it doppelgangs admirably, "certainly, sweet," it purrs "indubitably," familialy pecks and accepts pecks consecutively; pride to God, thanks. She's stiff-necked but it nuzzles her edges seethingly, a prince of numbness, a pain-absorbing fake suffering nobly the disillusionment of love like a made-for-TV stud, flickering, on peripheries, bracketed by Campbell's soup, while at the world's center you coolly by the fingers of your eyes peel words off the page and paste them to your brain, a flapless scholar and devotee; let us praise detachment, compartmentalization, inaccessibility, indifference of the heartless warrior to the side of his slaughtering—and the splintered man in the corner watching himself being slaughtered. Will not "break into blossom," the stepped out of body, but will absorb over-plus till blood. The Lord is a shepherd that maketh, no hand shall smite, he shall protecteth as of a wing over sorrow, shall be no heartquake in love's pressured jaw, nor green trepidation, and man shall walk away from his corpse.

1296

Doll wrestles the wet packed pectorals for dominance over man, pushes room in the maximus gluteus, shoves through the trapezius, kicks the latissimus dorsi like a rotten stump, clobbers the abdominals, stretches into the lexor hallucis longus, and spiders though fibers of the auricles and ventricles, powerfully, determined, sick of anonymity in the canned viscera of the machine; man clamps his perineum, locks his pectoralis major and minor, hardens beyond imagination his quadriceps and plantaris, and clasps his palmar fascia like a first round heavyweight subduing the insurrection of doll and retaining humanhood once again at Christmas. Doll struggles like a dying firework, invisibly again, shrinks into a BB sized inconvenience, hibernatorial and blind, somewhere around the bowels, while man responds infernally situationally to stimuli, shivers, perspires, weeps weakly at death, blisters at fire, psychologically unravels, driveling with protoplasm; doll is steel, invincible, forgiveless, dependent on pure whim, inexhaustible; man squirts cerebellum through automobile glass, welds skull skin to cratered cage, freezes numb, then black-to-amputation, pathetic loveblasted fragility one decimates with withdrawal of spasm or clam-close, while doll scans environment, eviscerates—or incorporates—indiscriminately, motiveless, leaving behind, let's say, the bighorn skeleton, the rabbit head, the pulsing heart, or conversely a supercharged psychopath as though Jesus-touched. The battle for callousness like Yosemite and Bugs, in a cloud, rages, out pops a canon, a glove, a mallet, a bomb in the crusade for supremacy, ongoing and indefatigable in the pupa-palpa-gastroenterologic world. Something is suddenly petrifying. Just yesterday man gazed with cold indifference upon a baby mammal.

1290

For my next, ladies & gentlemen, trick, I shall remove first this
hat, which I have for ten years through rain & snow adored,
never before human faces attempted I promise you thoroughly,
like this; then unpin, yes, my boutonniere, lay it—lovers—beside
the hat upon the sanatorium table; I spin it, thus—no hatches,
mirrors, boxes, fakes—so fresh like baby's chest my delicate
hat's chrysanthemum, drums suspense!, kliegs recompense!;
now unstrap that girdle my cummerbund—straightjacket, re-
straint—and flame it, thus, environmentalists: no charred rab-
bits or ducks, I assure; next, yes always a next before your
very dazzled pores, voila, my bow tie, that hangman's noose,
black & sinister butterfly upon the hat-and-flower slab; now
the mirrored showman's shoes—bovine canoes, coffins, ships—
flash, glitz, two side-by-side screams on the table; now my
simple rayon socks stuffed in mouths to stop the screams;
madams/gents glimpse my effeminate unmagical brackets;
the jacket next, arm, arm, liberated snakes, like a sail it flies,
look, off the stage; now the red French ruffled shirt, scler-
otic pierced stiff cardboard cuffs, sleeve, sleeve, untuck, off,
bare sandy colored hair, gaze upon skinny scholarly flesh;
unclasp, zip, heavy ankle-collapsed steam ship chimneys, I
kick off, catch, fold, reverently lay, stand before through
skewered powder blues like a centaur through a cloud,
bashful, pure, and clear; now the illusion begins. I climb
astronautically into the reinforced 3-inch-thick-wall plexi-
glass cube here raised off the stage on legs to prove no
amateur no trap door eschew; see me hazily inside, reddish
blue like a skinned vague deer behind rain streaked tears,
my windbags suck and bilge suffocating air, my toes squeal;

now the mixer, the dirty drum-turning mixer common
to construction bids you pass en route to soup, backs in
on black encrusted tires, hear sand & gravel grind, esquires
and slits, up close, magnified, harshly lit, like a blown out
knee, before it bilges grit down the chute, vomiting,
disgorging concrete to my feet, ankles, calves, thighs,
but as the solid gray Portland street covers my last fluff
of laundered hair encasing me in a petrifiable block I
am not here, I am there in the audience in the auditori-
um chair beside you and you and you and you plastered
emotionless frozen sealed incommunicative and unmoved.

1289

Money and God duke it out for supremacy. God says
"Moses, Abraham, Job, Rebecca;" Money draws "sustenance,"
like a gun. "Security," it fires, like Bill Hickok. "Power."
"Real Estate." "Monte Carlo." God spits. "Redemption,"
like a tommy. "Righteousness." "Compassion." Money
bloodies God's lip like Cassius. God reels backward
against an iron bench. Blotches on white robe. God
turns the cheek. Money crunches it like peanut butter.
God catches himself against rough bark, summons the
furies, and gut punches Dollar with brass knuckles,
upper cuts him on the chin. His nose pops like a water
balloon. Kick to God's balls; doubles; vomits. Boot
to rib. Grunts. Appendix malfunctions. Advantage mon-
ey: pushes God's face by hair into the fire. As coals
near king's eyes like thumbs adrenalin catapults Money
backward like a boulder; high arc kick by sandaled
foot, again groin kick, roundhouse, Tae Kwon Do
invisible machine gun, Money breaks into roses,
blackred nose ropes, teeth shatter. In annihilation's
vicegrip—such is the commitment to organismal surv-
ival—Money slices God with produced Egyptian dag-
ger; hand over gushing, lower right abdomen, slits
mouth into thigh, red lipstick, God catches in hand
blade lunging for heart, thumb hangs by bone; wren-
ches free knife, turns it like rocket, buries it to jew-
eled hilt through Money's masseter. Stunned, Mon-
ey, handle from jaw protruding, staggers, scrapes
against rock face, gazes into heaven; God watches
him scut like a claw-dragging crab. God warwhoops,

bloodsoaked and blue, "beggar," "abomination," mendicant," "fool," "artificer," "Mammon," "idol worshiper." Money, sitting zombie, crooks finger, confession; God, inching, forgiving, leaning in toward lip skin, flies backward into water, stomach blown open, both palms over hole, intestines, hydrochloric, lining, black bubbles, exit wound out spine, staring at the clouds. God, Money, like two boards fallen over, bases facing; in-between which and through march the masticating masses on either side of which, in the valley of the fools, the narrowest of passes, lays like two continuously disgorging wounds posterity's raw half-eaten carnage.

1269

God has a glisteny red mouth like a baby's and two gleaming new teeth. The round earth goes oblong as He sucks it like a tit. Plastic pants crinkle, poopies upon oopies, His pocket fatty legs protrude from animal tape. We call it tides but it's vacuum-lipped nipple and through it shoots cows, skyscrapers, Crisscrafts, coffins, avocados. He stiffens. He's almost always awake. Baby Boogums, Jack, and candlestick. Curds beside her, and whey. Oh my, oh my, what a gigantic boy am I. Nature roars and flows into his great big eyes. There had been such frictionlessness with mimosa, oleander, and such, before the thistle-punch. Angry Snookers. Had to change his nighttime Luvs. Frankly mama's exhausted, exasperated, mad, face awfully rumpled and hair gone kapow. Daddy's pissed as well, getting none, blasphemously regretting. God's mouth resembles sliced watermelon, cold vermillion crystals. Let us give Him clobber, pure pineapple clobber with heavy yellow custard, his first colostrum solid. Hand over forehead let us coalesce. Tree shredders flow through His pulsing lips. Baby's learning steps but crawls through calculus. S. S. S. We've erected something memoryless, North, East, South, West, clean, two sawn-apart beams, and enter stricken doors with quivering gargoyle tongue. Sinners, beggars, thieves Huey indistinguishably screams torrentially mean. Djibouti, The Crimean Sea, The Magellanic Straits, all geo-political-psychology split the flooding particulate with their infinitesimal statuary, pews, hymnals, and seed. It's epidemiological. The angry neonatal dictator, binky, blankey, and spew. Admit: it's weird. melon engapes maw, inhales, world puckers for the blow.

1262

Dear God: thank you for the physical beauty in the world, etc. and get fucked. Brutality festers under veneer. Abercrombie and Fitch and the other even-cornered orderly little boxes atop the cauldron of rage. I've read your absurd prevarications, burning bush, parting sea, water to wine, the whole bloody idiotic litany. What do you take me for? My son's in jail, my parents hate each other, and love is the biggest crock of shit in our world. Take it up the ass mr. big. I shove it in and squirt my ever-regenerating fascist through your anus. You "work in mysterious ways." Sure. Gotcha. Like multiple sclerosis, cerebral hemorrhage, schizophrenia, ovarian cancer, gang rape, endless battlefield slaughter, hunger and starvation, crack cocaine, mandatory economic survival, family annihilation, serial killer, christmas eve, the whole bloody genocidal mechanistic panoply of madness, demagoguery, power-lust, and blood papered over with The David, Notre Dame, Starry Night, The Cello Suites, The Divine Comedy, A Night at the Opera. You don't fool me with your poured concrete. The devil created you. Oops! a brief eulogy-interlude for my latest decimated friend—bone cancer—chemotherapy, steroids, morphine, marrow transplant—closed his lids on two blonde daughters, 9 and 13—hole in air, let me chant: HeyHeyHeyHey, HeyHeyHey, Hey, Hayi-o-ku-oo, tum tum. Thank you mr. zero for another picnic in the park. And he believed! But we know the irrefutable; invisible wasp with hypodermic stinger whirring through walls, money, steel, petition to jab it in the neck. "Come down, Come down, why dost thou hide thy face?" one frustrated poet begged. I will reveal. The mere hideous outline of you visible would decimate all animal hope or happiness. You think my personal circumstances blind and embittering? Don't make me laugh. I observe with microscopic scientific objectivity the botanical, zoological, and geological, and state with emotionless inanimacy the incontrovertible: I could wedge a baseball bat up your lower orifice, swing, and Hercules-hurl you to plague another planet-island of cripples and cruciality with your miracle-laden-liturgy and it would take a lifetime of restitution to clean the crap off the end of Louisville wood.

1253

I swallowed a quarter, 1997 D, Liberty, Washington, God,
eagle, choked like blowing enormous dick, it stuck along
shocked peristalses but worked, aching, to gut, leaving
me in despair. Dimes and pennies are kid's play, hors d'
oeuvres, half dozen slithered down like bays. Slid two coins
between eyeball and lid, antiquarian lobotomy, slit nerves.
Slipped in more filling brain with nickel and money-filth
finger prints touched with semen, shit, snot, vagina-juice,
making a cesspit of my head. Stuffed a twenty up my an-
us, then another, another, a knotted scarf of parchments,
three feet through the large intestine, licking the small, feel-
ing stuffed and desperate, but bank vault wealthy. The
nostrils proved problematic. I've seen Rinpoches thread
floss up one nasal cavity and down the other; I rolled
twenties together into twine and fed it in; behold, hang-
ing out my holes, horns! What remains? I had no fresh
slot-forming surgeries on my flesh. I chopped off my pen-
is and to the stump tied feed bag of money, like oats
to horse. The organic trash sack received the largess
of my circumcised love. Finally I employed my ten good
digits to crawl into the bath tub filled with singles from
my meaningless and withering family fortune, doused
the entire scene with kerosene, touched my nose to
a struck match head and called the conflagration rage.

1248

Confessions of a lunatic: Penises the size of psychological monsters buried in everywhichway presented female genitalia in a festering benedictine sabbath of procreation surrounded by icons, totems, and phalluses of copulation in a phantasmagoria of love, a delusion of love, lovesick, lovestruck, mooneyed biologies infinitesimally megalomaniacal microorganisms teeming and fizzing in the Petri dish of multiplication to Rachmaninoff or Def Leppard what gives a shit, imaginings of grandiosity and permanence veiled and trained under the blessings of God to some idiotic sober but intoxicating wedding march, the giddy bacilli or bacteria drawn forward through the quaint historical mountain town by double blind chestnut horses, "just married" scraped across the carriage eye, our saviors which shall plop forth from split silkiness conquering replications of the themselves, Harvard heroes or Julliard geniuses, their little sweetie pies swaddled in Jason's elusive fleece. Lawrence Livermore National Laboratory, the German National Laboratory for Heavy Ion Research, The Institut National de Physique Nucléaire et de Physique des Particules, Brookhaven National Institute for Nuclear Physics, The Indiana University Cyclotron Facility, The Bates Linear accelerator and collider, giants jutting through the clouds, Woton and Hunding protruding through cumulus their superior countenances, spectroscopy and monovalences flashing through their minds, linked by a double drop forged deep sea hook to Presidencies and Prime Ministers equally omnipowerful in the stratospheres, inaccessible as quasars, delusions of grandeur stiffening them with blood till they are hard as doors or Eiffel geometry, these puny pitiful electro-isotopic visigods prickling off Earth's rotundity like flaccid root hairs visible to the microscope, fuck them all their apocalyptic folderol, and their ever-worshiping wives dining at Cartier's.

The great powerful literary contemporaries I could name like death rattles by the hundreds: Rich, Schnackenberg, Lauderbach, Epstein, Lux, Economou, Valentine, Sobin, inmortales, maestros, hands like facial tissue, translucent Sampson Agonistes parting the reverentials like sorcery wanting to pick at the lint of their clothes, prophets, sages with the verbal acuity of pupa worm in tuxes at the National Book Award ceremony at the New York Sheraton sticking up like a miniature domino in dirt full of applauding and petit mal champagne sodden minds, the devil take them all to the cauldron of no alphabet at the sulphur erupting pit of the inferno's hungry gut. Coldwell Banker's one hundred top performers—the Platinum Club—at Belagios with their Audemars, Vacherons, or Roger Dubuises, bronze, polished, inculpably genuine, the woman understatedly magnificent and generally plus-sized like pouted sage grouse dabbed in rouge, at the pool, the tables, the shows, the beds getting a little extra-curricular cold-call commissionless fun, mutually admiring the diamond shaped Plexiglas platinum award each received at the plenary banquet one by one like diplomates, may each reproduce themselves by a billion, fuse, and ascend like a misty cloud of the brokers extraordinaire to the 30,000 sq. ft. mansion in the sky of Peter Neederman, Pres. and CEO of Coldwell Banker Worldwide, sleeping like a goat protruding satyr after multiple masturbations on his boil infested ass. But I crashed out half-wit, mentally handicapped, my medulla oblongata, a.k.a., my spinal bulb juiceless and infantile, a dwarf and rather hideous to gaze upon, slightly thalidomide, so forgive me my rage, my indescretion, my vulgarity, my plain misinformation, but I fail—and have always failed— to appreciate the difference between man and grass.

1223

Last night sprouted splotches of silver pelt, howled and stank, tasted bitter bark of birch (high horizontal parallel tooth marks), sprayed liquid gold east and west, north and north, steam, relief, snow, exhalation, cracked twigs underfoot, moonless dark, rushing brook, whiff of snow-fertility, shook robotical mechanical abnormalities at the base like earthquaking cartoon rectangles and squares, lines jittering into each (society's migraine), paced, paced, draping-shirt above dangling sex, naked legs, Best Friend crushed-fleece mocs, wife floating above in bed, marshmallowed, neat, toes Palmolived and translucent—cuticles and pink quarter-moon shoals—husband beyond high dark-stained walls on uneven squishiness shaky, spindly, groping, half-stumbling, pelvic equilibrium on unfamiliar terrain, coyote operetta from distant tribe plaintive-flying into heart veins, grabbing ventricle and auricle like handfuls of clay and flinging them up up into the nebula, both within my cavity and without, a double thing beating, beating alive as a star. Three AM, the austere never sleeping granite peaks spearing God's spleen invisibly gathered round my waves—congregation of indifferent believers—witnessing a soft squeamish inculcated sack of underbellied humanity shed his ghostliness and smear the dung and nitrogen rich earth upon his globe and hair and neck, fur bald flesh in dust of dirt, paint skunk scat across his chest, and drive drive madness into the flesh of life with buck like flanks, with flank of stag, coiled and sprung, cloven, tucked and flung. He has piled upon the ground a mansion for flies, wrigglers, burrowers and bugs and shall re-enter his studded cube wherein resides the tub and bowl, is half-way there, a coyote-to-human supernatural blur. A naked hand emerging from fur down-pushes the handle. After passing through the transforming shaver of home's threshold leaving behind a mound of bristles, a naked man closes the door, punctuates with shadow the lampless light, slips in bed beside his wife, curls into a muscle memory of animal, and spectacular with echoes of elementalism sleeps until graininess extinguishes night.

1221

Assume a keen and precise perception, stropped like a razor, assume he sees sharp as fish gills detail, and it torments. Assume he perceives the bottom drawer pinching a bit of sleeve sticking out like a blister from perfect pine. Assume this flaw assassinates sleep. Assume he stares all night at walls refusing to repair the human failure. Assume he is under a doctor's care. Behavior modification. Sitting in anxiety. Pools. Pools. Assume an awareness of a thousand imperfections. A stain in his anus. A light switch half off. A toilet seat tottering on its point like a diamond preparing to crash. Assume a brain fire. The stomach acid eating the shale of his spine shall push through at three hungering for fuel. The dark burns his eyes. Assume an uncanny tendency toward catastrophe. Death by insomnia, extinction by responsibility. Assume perpetual wakefulness inside a spider-wrapped bundle reserved for future hunger, rolled within fiber of blanket plastered with enzyme. Imagine a hyper-awareness of the bladder, hands, and phlegm suppressing L-tryptophane from filling the brain. The man wrings soul, prays, paces, feigns sleep in a kind of cataleptic trance. Imagine he claws his face. Imagine an onslaught of self-recrimination. The man is honorable, dependable, sweet, every breath exhaled a monumental defeat. The minute hand smashes the next groove like an anvil. This is Odysseus opening his flesh to wind like a shirt, the wind stings his blood, freezes raw flesh like Mennen skin bracer, an alcohol splash driving him out into paradise. Assume he imagines he is lying naked upon a white table. His psyche sprouts in every direction the impenetrable thousand knives of perception. Asp. Mechanical porcupine.

Mediaeval glove crawled off the hand. Assume a protection so categorical, totalizing, ubiquitous, and complete that it stings the man into the blind annihilating crucifixion of belief.

1220

Again the taut monofilament line between fisherman and fish, gossamer, glimmering, three pound bull red and two hundred pound bastard battling in salt biliousness, fucker c'mon, come home to daddy, ink-blot tail-muscle flicking in granite green, gills pumping, mouth-cartilage refusing, two animals in opposite atmospheres cut by the scissors of surfaces, glass sheet, almost plexiglas, 10 lb test sunk through like solid sculpture, bronze, at the outdoor art mart beside the thrashing sailfish, contest, wills, death, nourishment, fresh red blood, the man early forties, stubble beard, business failure, two kids, raven haired wife-bitch, tortured with cratering fantasies of wealth, accolades, ribbons, oral sex, congratulatory boxes, Europe, the fish Executive Vice-President, Ben Franklin Life & Casualty, fat, bald, sweaty, heavy drinker—Black Label—swinger, fertilizer of thousands, clogged floater valve, this hook in throat, block and tackle punishment yanking him to hell the foreordained testamental destiny of the sacrilegious, barb in poppers, swift intractable Adjudicator, some are fouled through back or tail, unfair, but the souls of all infidels are ripped from guts to float unredeemed and eternally in the upperworld; the man: Orthodox, gold icon wearer, the only wholeness known is this standing upon the sloughs in an inch thick fiberglass bowl, Mercury outboard, live shrimp, Embassador Abumatic casting reel, singing to himself, hauling up spam, the bump, the strike, the exhilarating instant the magnificent beast breaks surface into the steel gray light, whopper!, giant!, mother of trout! swivel and claw with shrimp bits still attached removed from lip, the man cold refreshing drafts, it doesn't arrive higher than this;

the fish: nihilistic, savage, mean as shit, shitting, a lifetime of stuffed resentment and rage croaking out his mouth as he lays upon mates in the red, blue, and silvery slime pit, fry me you hypocritical bloodless white robed priest-cowards on your Neptune-thrones, double standard bastards clinging to cleanliness like a culture of dweebs, translucent phosphor sacs flaring pure emerald green, gluttonless, fornicationless, covetousless, hedonisticless slipping through cubes like a breathing death, tuna-fresh. The man: loved but slaughtered the wife's raw eggs his whips slammed into, wiped until wringing guilt with their hearts and spills of shame with their hair, the fish issues cackles of cynicism from his chair, eradicating the blight the man throws the switch with holocaustal delight on his cold creel of criminals.

1215

Stopped my mouth with cement and trowel, did the Bible
from prayer, no faith in that creature God, Dog, Odg,
like a white porcelain john I am, a drilled-of-pulp tooth
enamel-sealed, mason made, dentist formed, the Bible
a bottlestopper in the anus, puttied up pores, now I
choke, ganglanded, oblong sick screams of help to
Catholics, Jews; lashed to chair, brutalized, released
with dried white concrete orifices, with scissor snapped
synapses, full of Ecclesiastes and Thessalonians brain
like cat-clawed ball, I am crawling, crawling in stun-
ned unreception, solid massive toilet, God filled you
with daddy who filled daddy with me, mother you
were there with your black rimmed miracle tube,
sorcery zapped, cracked with glitter, lightning zagged
out sky into you, hurled by masculine divinity, chan-
nelled birth violence, witnessed angry revolution,
fertility madness, omnipowerful unavoidable Pres-
ence; the testament binds me like brick bowels, cheese
and tree wood, I petrify through the regal and tow-
ering land, the mesmerizing eyes, the vitality strands,
the royal cataracting blood gorges of the beautiful
and sad, once a breathing gaping hole, I grey among
the statuesque, pattering wet Portland block, the
Word a rock embedded in macrame beside a rock,
linearly, a necklace of rocks through the esopha-
gus into the gut, swallow, swallow, razors of gall
and kidney, star-stuck. I shall stand sandaled in
muck in a hail of prepuces, sulphur, and toads, all
spring-summer without slumber or lust looking up
like a tulip, like rust petals, an iron truss. The stick
you see lavishing branches shall be me in ecstasy.

1199

The whole fish skeleton fine as angel hair, as asbestos thread,
the transparent rib-fan, the spine, the pinkish head, the jaws
and razor teeth, flounder-oval, delicate, a coin of pins and
needle, floats before my eyes in grainy light like a negative
in air, wispy clean, unblemished, without sand or bill, speci-
min perfect. Why? This morning. The blinds closed. A mil-
ky hovering snowy light. These are not my bones. My heavy
bones. My mammoth skull. My mastodon pelvis. My ulna
and radius. My patella and swords. My femur and coccyx.
My phalanges and metatarsals. This little trout. This milli-
pede. When I die the world will know bones. With no poems
stuck to them, with no sexual flesh between. No red and
blue sherbert. No pudding afloat in bowls. The world shall
know pure massive calcium monument, testamental, absol-
ute. Bones that loved. Bones of masturbation. Bones of
no deadly god. Bones that flamed a wall of fire. White clean
bones uncremated up no flue but lying bare in glitter soil,
eye holes huge as cannon bore. Flagpole without flag. Patrio-
tism without grit. Bones of cat, skunk, or rat; possum or
mutt, furious, fixed grimace of fear or hate, decomposed,
bits of fur, are beautiful wadded experiments, paper drafts,
noble as plaster, paste, or rubber cement to these Ajax,
Apollo, Prometheus, and Hercules crumbling towers. Well,
fuck it. Nobility blows. Just the bones of cowardice, capitu-
lation, squeamishness, crucifix, mollusc bones, bones of
squid, bones of jellyfish and octopus. These were mine and
yours and yours. Programed. Scriptural. Heroic countersquirt.
This ichthyonosaur floating before my nose, neon pulsing,
psychedelic, iconographic Christ piper-prophet fossilized
upon the mind to guide us from our unction like a flame.
Rising from these lines I trip over the Sistine chapel of a fly.

1197

He departed without food for he did not need
food. The third day he was strong as the second
and the forth tolerably erect followed by the
fifth of solid walking across hot sand, staff in
hand, and then the seventh, goat skin dangling
dust-dry, feet blistered, tongue eating air, licking
God, the eighth, the ninth, a transcendence, a
blessing, he did not glow but needed no susten-
ance like common biologies, floated above the
flame, chosen, focused with resolve, walked to
a Promised Land methodically supernaturally
but a man just a man replete with belief, tenth,
fifteenth, slept under dippers, drinking thought,
philosophy, ignorance, innocence, thirty days,
thirty-nine days without sex or food, without
love or lye, without Jesus or Mary, a young
man with Michalangelo toes, a loin cloth, a rag,
wandering, wandering, steady as she goes, like
a prow plowing grain, no one worshiped him,
none prayed to him, nor did he pray, stunned of
prayer by rage and death, on the fortieth he did
not die nor weep nor sing nor stay but ate the
sudden blackness of locusts hilariously clacking.

1191

The glorious night, the sumptuous night, the night of turkey stuffing and eating, of fat drippings, of soft meat pulled apart in strong hands, baked and hot, the longed for night engorged with champagne, strawberries, and walnuts, and white iced cake, the risen night, enmounded, slippery with oil, globed in halves, hemispherical, packed with butterfingers; the blind fish night, the nosing mullet night, the night of blunt bumping, scary and inexplicable, the night of dark foreskulls and double-twisted bones, the night of torn lamb's meat soft as smooth pullet, starring the print-whorls; the night of tuxedos, chrysanthemums, and seances and hammering whales' backs; the death night, the coffin night, the night of burning nails, the night of the baby in the sarcophagi, curled and tight; the night of flamingoes and reeking pelicans standing on the open eyes, the night of blue horses flying overhead; it is the night for executing witches with knives and gasoline and eating their charred esophagi; the night of condiments; the night of breakage in a too powerful fusion, of lace and luster bombs, of broken packages and escaping tadpoles, the delectable pie-night, scallop crusted, thumb and elbow crusted, blue juice-bubbling; the night of forests and switches, forests and loam beds, the dream-twitterers tucked under leaf comforters, the night of fairies, dwarfs, and flitterers, chins upon the bed's edge, repositioning pump strings, in camouflage-fatigues, earth smeared faces, loaded with missile trajectories; the night of boa constrictors, cold and draping, of crawling vines and white crinolines, the night of slimy smears on pure materials at the midriff level and the hemline, of slugs, earthworms, and millipedes slithering in, turning up clay like a screwplough; the night of multi-pledgings consisting of three fingers, four knees, and two spines rocking upon the calcium moon clothed in blood clothed in veins clothed in sails wedged in the shape of self in air, explicit, delimited, yet exponentially grand like the firmament on a wizard's hat; the night of lip licking lusciousness no frog shall shit upon nor lizard stink until the fiery knife blazes a glistening slice off the ground like the bleeding flesh off a cantaloupe rind.

1179

First I prepare the face with a warm wash rag by soaping off every grain of make-up, not one speck of lipstick, eyeliner, mascara, pancake base; then Witch Hazel-saturated cotton balls deep in eye creases, ear canals, folds and seams until they blacken like baseballs; I have already washed the hair, squeezed it free, toweled it dry, blown it with air, brushed it to sheen (I prefer raven black), and tied it off to expose the neck. Here vulnerability drips like rose petal tears and my tongue pulls to lick the white alabaster and gold tones, but I restrain my animal lust, treat her with utmost dignity. Next, I wash fingers free of Revlon, soil, and earthly dust till soft pouches of blood under cuticles shine like plums oozing yet contained in transparent skin. I swab between the fingers, brush the nails, and delicately rub in circular fashion along the grooves of print whorls. I have already slipped off in suds the wedding ring and placed it like a crown upon a pure linen towel alongside her gold Seiko and heirloom hair brush. Similarly, I have cleansed her teeth, submerging the floss under the gum, flicking free food bits and plaque such that blood strives to ooze small red pearls which with tissue I swipe from inside her soft crevasse until like sap they shut off at the insignificant irritation tap. Then I remove blouse and bra and employ alcohol to swab the aureOAS, each individual hair round the lunar flow, under the globes where salt lines appear pushing them up and over with hands guaranteeing sterility, and again I repress the centrifugally pulling suck of my open lips in exchange for the parabola of decency which few human males possess in the presence of inert nude femininity. Then I pull down the panties as if popping from the oven a done cherry tart, slip them past ankles folding them acceptably like some kind of soft crab, but this time I trade the fire of alcohol for soapy terrycloth, running it up carefully after folding it round with a gentle release her coarse springy hair, like oiling the blueblack steel of a Remington gunbarrel, then pat it dry till all beads dissolve and the engorged red vulva glows like cataract covered with fern. Slowly with spatula palms under buttocks I turn her and into her pores push impregnated frankincense, ambergris, and myrrh until t he globes resemble moonlit isinglass, almost platinum, almost gold. And now, omitting here detail of the few remaining ceremonials, she is ready: pure nakedness, pure the aforementioned vulnerability, pure magnificence, every arm hair sparkling, every vein standing, every plate and shield saddle-soap softened. Efficiently, I take exactly what I need from the tray—nothing more, nothing less—having already, between the bath and the instruments switched on a CD (I have always enjoyed the passion of Rachmaninoff), and in the gray, her body still posteriorly positioned, with a votive candle haloing her head facing northeast, I begin to partake.

1176

When the bullets zinged off institutional walls into the con queso pot and hotdog bin; when the plastics exploded in the parking garage sending truck pieces whizzing like satellites, when the size 38D breast swallowed a .9mm slug down the back of its esophagus and out the other side wide as an elephant's trunk; when the teeter totter, the tether ball, and concrete box sprung mangled pomegranates of human blood matted with hair and rainbow entrails; when the wife's face stuck to the pillow with the smoking black hole and the bedsheet underneath; when 8 ft. up every faux drywall dripped ruby red struggle marks, and below one such edifice slumped two soaked bundles, father and son, with sticky notes straightpinned to each: "revenge"; when among the copper and turquoise river-rush and blunt nosed fish in white-gold sun-needles and moon-dark threads, current-rolled like a broken Ken, the environmentalist's head; when howitzers inside the wild horses' chests blew them into hamburger in a New Mexican field, banquet for birds; when a shovel discovered a pretty Herzegovinian mound to be a fresh blister of skulls; when a razor sharp stretch of Jasper, Texas, asphalt tore off chunks of blue-black skin and apocalyptic gore dragged by rope behind a confederate truck, like hanging living spitwads on a rural classroom ceiling, or plastering storm-strewn newspaper on a chain link fence; when what terrified the crows from a Wyoming corn field banquet was a bludgeoned and naked homosexual; and finally, when in the janitor's bathroom the cackling police officers plunged the toilet of a Haitian prisoner's anus with the handle of a plumber's helper I slid into her slippery flesh and she arched up to deepen the thrust and we both tore out heavy clay scoops of air with our sharp cry and moaning throat simultaneously as if two Earths collided, spewed upward and intermixed forming a new harmonious planet.

1158

Sewed two cat heads onto my chest for breasts, black, whiskered, one chartreuse, one amber eyed, mouths fixed in terror-grimace (decapitated them alive, naturally); fixed a pig snout into my crotch for cock, raw, red, jagged, but eternally erect; coconut shell pieces for kneecaps. hairy but tough and sexy; casava skins for butt enhancement, smooth, pettable, delicious, pale; slivered banana peel for hair, long curvy strips with a lilt like a soccer star; the cat stomachs doubled as moccasins and the pig gut made a fine scrotum wrapped round two whole hazelnuts, hanging. Needed a new heart and decided the ripe red plum, so pried my cavity with a surgeon's vice and stuffed it in, veiny, glutted, sugary-sweet, dripping deep red streaks mosquitoes could swill on sweltering moonless afternoons; a scooped-out lemon rind for bladder and blown out egg shell for chin, the kind I smeared Paas over on Easter and called it art, beaming like a watt; bathed in compost to the crown, stuck on pheasant and buzzard feathers to ready myself for she for whom I am cooking shrimp Mozambique with coconut milk, cayenne pepper, and Rachmaninoff, she whom by my creole-smooth telephone voice accepted my invitation sight unseen—the Personals, you know—and who I am positive will be wearing for playful aperitif thong panties with the window I've seen in nudy magazines. Decided from ear lobes, to dangle one live goldfish each by needle holes punched through gossamer fins, a touch, an accessory as Paloma Picasso would declare, with a smattering of close-to-surface-blood wrist cologne. I have such a beautiful clean-angled house, roomy, high-ceilinged, everything squared, spacious, shiny, flat, lacquered, and wide, and I inside, part ichthyologically glittering, part vegetatively glammed, mythological, nightmarish, a creature no woman could refuse.

1154

And this little piggy squealed "no,no,no,no," all the way home. And then all the toes were accounted for: the big, the middle, the nondescript, nondescript's neighbor to the East, the itty-bitty which made baby laugh like a nautilus. And then the toes blinked out like a disappearing photograph, and baby went on a miniature vacation to Puerto Vallarta where a lion almost devoured him like a fortune cookie, but he escaped and wind rattled the blinds like dangling bones, and he whimpered and whispered a prayer-precursor to the Divine Death Overture, something about soft protrusions and blue rain. And baby Carroll decided he was having none of it and shattered two panes in the living room belonging to Daddy and his entourage one of whom played the Ace of Spades and raked in the kitty while on the artery a flying mechanical scream engulfed horizontal human moans in a white steel cube smudged with a red intersection and far, far away two events happened simultaneously: an imaginary Holstein jumped over an idiot moon keeping constant vigil on the continuous catastrophe, and in the silo accompanied by secret platoons of yellow anthropods Jack finally found Jill's gooey ooze representing nucleic acid's undeniable invincibility.

1136

These are the grotesqueries: long fake fingernails painted purple glued on the end of bitten fingers used to enter minute streams of data into a PC; a bent and contorted rubber man giving himself a blow job on a chintz bedspread at mid-day behind heavy curtains to a whirring traffic sound in a moderate-sized Midwestern town reeking of sanitized industrial smells and environmental mediocrity, sucking like a pig his red dong, snorting and slurping until the gun fires hot flan into his rasping mouth; two average boobs "anesthetized upon a table" swelling like birthday balloons as the Master slips silicon heavy pouches into slits wide as orgasm-grins, the kind that closes you like a briefcase and slams a Charlie horse into your thighs, two massive mounds rising from ash topped with bright red hard proud maraschino cherries; a half dozen frosted orange vials lining the medicine chest like circus milk bottles daring to be bowled over, one for nerves, one for insomnia, one for anxiety, one for bipolarism, one for rage, and one for love—a puppet theater with a silver curtain behind which reside Princess Penelope, Queen Prunella, Poh-Poh the Clown, Hrothgar the dragon and the dastardly Count Badunov each with their respective handmaidens, henchmen, and courtesans, all attired in peaked white caps and the family crest across which is written the prescription for victory; splatting a human brain against the broad part of a bat, particularly if the scalp is Black and the bat has four running legs attached to and pinwheeled by a common hip, whose politics ends with the word "premicist," if you get my drift, in Bama, Tejas, or Mississip, the bat electrical taped for grip and discolored with consistently smacked grand slams against opponents under floodlights to cheering stands, flashbulbs blinding the victor with grandiosity and capturing on

silver the beautiful slaughter; O the grotesqueries are these:
shoving the middle finger to the ham-knuckle up the anus of
a cat, the cat a frozen sculpture of horror, in the guest room be-
side the closet and wall-socket into which is jammed a light bulb
a lamp a black rubber chord and a two fingered hand; the armless
drummer grinning under moustache in a smoky dome full of booze,
babes, Cobras, and panthers, one strumpet who from a distant pew
coats his body with lust as the cymbals clash, the snares and traps
intensify a rap so hot nothing connects the sticks to his stump but
blurry air or a heat-mirage whose dust flies round a fool diving in;
sinking surgical gloves through fascia and muscle, ligatures and
sheath and striking pure granite, like boulders sunk in silt, granite
arteries, granite gut, granite lungs, granite pump, rock upon rock
in soft mud, immovable, great hereditary tumors imbedded and
petrified into heavy, cold, dead, blunt, blind, unemotional stone.

1113

I have decided I will do this: I will eat my father.
I will cook him to tar and spoon the goo; I will
melt his shoulder bones into his buttocks and
watch his eyes boil like eggs. I own the kettle—
cast iron—and the site, a barn alive with mice and
bats, abandoned, dilapidated. I will stab him
severally, split his wishbone, and boil him til his
brain snakes through. Then the fun! I will eat
every atom of him over years until I have swal-
lowed, digested, and eliminated my father. I will
spice my meals with cranium filings. He will
reappear in the water supply as the rationale
for Perrier! After that who cares! Let them fry
me. Let them waste ink and trees. Let others,
righteous to the pips, over oatmeal, snap off
their lips long balloons of diatribe, the loyal
pets of their shoe-tassels waiting. I will have
achieved my goal, liberated to song, no longer
man but soul. Prosecute the doll of my body,
bloodhound me down, convict me like an SS
man, let the pellet fizz. You cannot kill God nor
an empty robe. When in death my neck sinks
down know that what passed through it in grainy
chunks, savoringly masticated, enspirited me,
peeled back filth to liquid gold, made me beautiful.

911

After binging on Dreyer's butter pecan in a period of weight gain I went upstairs and almost forced myself to throw up. I gazed into the toilet like Narcissus. I imagined slamming two fingers down my throat till a Vesuvius roared. I felt the weeping of my stomach, and my accusatory belt. I wanted to kill the monster in me, the cowardice, the unceasing executioner. Downstairs I heard the John Wayne movie: the charging bugles, the beating of horse hooves, the swirling commotion of rifle fire and expiration, all muted by a series of walls and corners, and in my soft cube, wondered. I knew that finally I was tortured not enough to perforate the tissue of my gut, that I was still a bit of an hibiscus, that I would rejoin unpunctured my partner in the film. This brief lavatory interlude was brought to you by Glamor Magazine, self hatred, pitiful parenting, powerlessness, and a rare form of male bulimia.

827

I strip the raised vein out my forearm by lifting it
whole with the blade of a knife and with it make a
ball of yarn I call my son. Like spaghetti spun on
a fork, thick and high and standing on its own wide
base, I give him eyes, a name. Allan I say, Allan.
The ball glistens red like tomato sauce. Say "Daddy,"
I command and feed him apricots. Say "Master."
The wrapped vein self-perpetuates and renews
by squirting and sucking in a ceaseless repetition of
sleep and food. Say, "I am your nemesis or life dup-
licate. I am your acolyte fashioned to echo your
productivity. I will assume the presidency." I
do not miss the vein that became my son though
it left a tunnel in my flesh for he is me watery and
splashing my stupendous trail. God love him.
God give him meat. Give him feet to incinerate.
I spin my child like a plate of vermicelli and he
quivers, smiles, accumulates—but then he hates,
the procedure awry, me, the plate, the fork, the
sea contained within the vein like a stiff steel pipe
of hell, he digs, he spits, he smolders, he flies, and
eyes two slit exposures of spite attempts to die.

816

Am I more like steel or fruit inside. If you drilled deep through me would I finally break your bit or ooze pear-meat and weep like a godless Jesus of Nazareth? I want to know. Drill me to the core. Scew out big chunks of me in your deep steel grooves and spit me free, you with your blindness and vulnerability. Make me spasm and curl with your all-nighters and narcomania my teenage son. Find my vanadium or peach-pear-plum blood. You have drilled through my flesh, it flew apart like a burn, and several inches into the beams in my bones, but I'm still steadily beating. Push hard on your tool. Drill through my collar past my lungs into my heart pushing with all your weight, feet off the ground, grinding out meat; find what's there. Get to my meddle. Drop out. Coke up. Fuck the syringe. Find your own gore in vehicular winter. Am I cold? Am I mechanical? Can I walk through closed windows? If you peel back my surfaces do I glisten? This is your mission. Let me see from a distance the crack pusher's wing fold over your shoulder and usher you forward, your two backs fusing. Let me witness dissolution. It is the father's privilege. To strip off my sirloin like meat off a prey to find what's lying inside my cage. Let me see graphically what your brain isn't getting: high school teacher's spittle, orange lunch room chile, that geeky conventional gangly comaraderie, auditorium pep rallies, an appropriate foreign language, stupidity, time, time, time.

716

Each molecule of sea water is a number, randomly
connected into other numbers in all shapes and attitudes,
combining, colliding, merging, and fusing, the sea
a googoplex of numbers, intermixed, overlapped,
forming an undulating organism, rising and falling,
swelling, swaying. Many a human has drowned in
numbers, inhaling 10s and 7s, their last appendage
a raised hand sliding under. The combination of numbers
form sea colors: aquamarine, green, copper, brown—
colors that weave one's breath into bursting, birds
loosed upon the air which are themselves numbers,
3 birds, 46 birds, 328 bursting birds, 2476 birds forming
a cloud whose molecules are numbers. Nitrogen,
hydrogen, oxygen numerals forming the sweet face
of a colt, a colossus, or cow floating, and metastasizing.
One cat sleeps on my lap, 2 squirrels quarrel in the
trees, 3 pans hang from metal hooks, 4 trucks wheeze
down the street. The tongues, lips, and teeth of
children at Eisenhower Elementary School form in
unison the sounds of numbers. Count to 10. Bob
can do it! Wendy can do it! Jason can do it, too!
Numbers bouncing off the walls, doubling back,
and filling classroom, save a few which slip through
cracked windows, like ecstatic criminals. I love you.
You plus me equals love. 1+1=2 or 3 or 5, who
plus 3 generations equals 71. Fourteen people of
mixed gender wait on the curb in the year '97 or
was it '61? Mine is tied with a four-in-hand. Seven
steps; a landing, 7 steps, a landing; 7 steps, a landing;

every other one 45 a degree turn left to a door on
each of 18 floors, counts the man with OCD. There
will be a minimum of 6 and a maximum of 16 chemo-
therapy treatments beginning every 3rd Monday
and lasting 3 hours each. She died at 63 after working
40 years. The system on which I compose these lines
has 32 megabytes of RAM, a 4.3 gigabyte hard
drive, a 1.44 diskette drive, a 56 K fax modem, 4
megabytes of video memory, a 3-D virtual memory,
an AC-3 camcorder, a 600 x 300 DRI printer with
a 100 page sheet feeder, a 7 resistant fax, and a
266 MHZ Pentium processor chip. On the tip of
my last going under finger, thrust high: 1angel flickers.

641

There's always another woman. There's always another mate.
There's always another penis or vagina. Another conquest.
Another salve. There's always another euphoria. The vodka
bottle with its pretty label, full and standing up. The lovely bour-
bon. The ivory skin. The freckled skin. The dune above the sex.
The fullness. The gratification. The slake. The God-power.
The worshiping. The praying to. The stiff icon vibrating in
space she bows to, breeze drawing across it. It's name. It's
puppet-ness. It's tip. To lie back flooded, rushed, eyes
closed, forgiven. With disconnected legs floating. Arm
around a neck. There's always the beautiful fluid, clear,
warm, amber, black, heady, the sexy bottle, the mouth,
the lip, the high-class image, the wheatfield logo, the promise,
the despair. There's always the entertainment and distraction,
the series, the bowl, the cup, the trip, the sunskin, the movie,
the sweeping away, the dulling, the home devoid of you,
the divan empty, the floor waiting, the house weeping,
the truth knowing. There's always the moment without
you in it. She was a babe. Wow. Breasts! She loved it.
She did everything. Slim-hipped. You should have been there,
it just kept flowing. They creamed 'em, 21 points, a rout.
I'm practically hoarse. It took six hours to get there,
she was all over him, there were three private bedrooms.
And overdrive. There's always a flawless waxed clean
new car, smart, blissed. There's always the funeral dirge
for the old, junked, and the game card, the scratch it off,
the jackpot, the instant God, pricked with gold, dipped,
the immortality and the wither. The manicure and big shot.

There's always the tree, the rock, the sea, the moon
and stars, the broadcasts, the races, the channeling, the
controlling external mind which sucked out your brain
to servitude, the blizzard, the absence, the where you're not,
the infinite superior exhilarating intoxicating exotic locations
not feeding you, the counting, the numbers, the fear,
the ten digits making millions, the plague of flies. There's
always the television. The little three foot high flogger.
There's always the knuckle in the eye. The dominance and
execution, poof!, you're gone. The mass murder. That's
the best, the slaughtering with a sub-machine gun
everyone at Luby's while they're eating, trays and blood
flying. The lie. The lie. The million ways of transmuting, re-
fusing, and not acknowledging the simple fact of self-disgust.
watts flicker and plot his demise. They feel like they
are smeared with shit and want a hose. They feel the shit
of shame and want to bath in soapy loam. When the father is
sleaze-duplicitous life's soul cracks and fluids leak like a
ball of grease which drives the all, and from the depths crawl
the arthropods—skeletal, thoraxic, hard-shelled, dragging heavy
sacks of mud—to swarm the tides of sewage-crud, crawl
thickly like a blowing foam to eat the world's carcass clean.

631

Well, I heard that this death row inmate has allowed science to slice his lethally injected corpse into single millimeter strips, every organ scanned, muscle upon muscle, his body filleted into innumerable sheets thin as Kleenex, for the examiners, a CAT scan of his entire disinherited body. Rape won't appear, homicide won't dash between the molecules. We won't find child trauma crouching behind garages, crying. But meat will glisten, like freshly sliced veal, a Hubble scan of grain and ganglia, calcium and tissue, the ultimate visible man. You could make a board game of this, a card game of concentration, what strip follows strip, what strip yearns for strip, you could award money for being close on an anatomical-geographical map: the Country of Pulmonaria, The Cardiac Republic, The Reproductive Coast, your strip draped over your arm, like fresh pasta. The man died for his sins—rape, dismemberment—but lives inside the instruments. Well, it just caught my eye, something I heard from a friend in passing, embedded in a wider conversation about competitiveness, superiority, dominance, etc.,the criminal lurking in my mind after escaping her lips. Grotesquerie curls in the routines. If time were a ground-to-sky wave pushing forward, while you in your circumscribed space were down-shifting into first, elsewhere some technological saw was subdividing a man whom they froze solid first. Now I am a literary agent in the basement of my home with a bone-white phone, a flickering computer, pens like bottle rockets in a cup, crammed book shelves, and, dare I admit it, a stuffed Beagle pup. I rub my eyes. I feel the thickness of my hands. I see my thighs aswirl with hair sweeping to my knees, and knee caps like helmets. I sit in a chair, or wander up the hundred 2 x 4 boards builders years ago hammered into stairs, to feel the sun, my fingers through my hair. And you my love are . . . somewhere . . . browsing, eating, day-dreaming, most likely working, drawn around yourself, like a bedsheet full of treasure and tied at the top, one beautiful piece. It's not enough to declare, "and round and round she whirls in space," referring to Earth, like a colossus unfolding, head in the sky, a stock response. We must return to this: a criminal who willed his heft to science, the science itself, electronic saws, weird obsessions, the immortality-drive, rape and dismemberment, the mackerel thrashing of too-tight lives, the infinite capacity of the human mind to escape prison walls and mundanity, the beauty of minutiae and the machinery to enter it, God, galoshes and slickers within which to slip as we examine the blood-sherbert which was man.

630

Watching professional ice hockey on TV, the semi-finals, Detroit
vs. Colorado—brutal, clean, elemental, fast, steel on ice, ripping—
the kind of thing I like to track, like a leopard in grass the
microscopic movements of its prey, like to pretend I'm tiger in
the blades calculating, watching, fangs tasting blood, like to
imagine I'm on my couch sublime, amber-eyed, sleek, and wise.
Never mind the commercials for beer or automobiles, those
false interludes, those insignificant blips between magnificence,
no bigger than grains, never mind mini-pauses in the beast
which flows. I'm a beautiful animal, efficient, quick, my brain
transmits down the length of my skin, this Saturday night wide
with silk flashes of heat, my mate in the grotto nearby soft
and ready on the inside. That's hockey, a tail of star-dust
following a puck-like-a-comet to the score-zone, wham!
I'm all cat and blood-in-the-heart of the players when suddenly
a dead squid wrapped in blue ribbon fills the screen, a wet,
veined, whole, big squid wrapped in ribbon dead on the ice
someone snuck in probably under his shirt and hurled there,
a proud ocean squid, glistening, maybe still full of eggs
or fertilizer, maybe wise. I know almost zero about squid,
but I thought of soft, grey-mauve sacks, of suction cups,
of syncopated pulsing through water, of ink clouds, of eyes
half-buried in slippery skin. I thought of the indignity of not
being eaten, instead being thrown into a stadium of screaming
fans after a propitious score, the scoreboard flashing WIN!
WIN!, eyes glassed over and tentacles lashed, the indignity of
ending up in an arena and then the trash, the waste. I stood
in my human flesh—bald tufts of hair, soft dick, clawless
hands—just rose off my butt, not panther, ocelot, cougar, nor

lynx, and, remote control limp in hand, looked at this jarring sacrilege. What happened next is hard to explain. Forty-eight years of advertisements flew through my brain: gleaming teeth, shiny legs, silky hair, quenched thirst, needless speed, satiation, dominance, self-righteousness, the whole sewer-marketplace. I cannot say what I mean. Body parts appeared before my eyes—lips, napes, knees, hips, tit-cleavage, flat midriffs, like an oar-shattered lake, all swirled into a grotesque human ball laced with TV's stupid predicaments, situations, blowings away, exonerations, manipulations, mechanical tittering, skits, extravaganzas, and routines. And small explosions occurred on the surface of my skin, eruptions through which broad shafts of light ripped, stutterings and decompositions, burnings and disintegrations, breakdowns of the internal circuit board of me, profoundly, as if I were a melting lid around an inextinguishable eye—clear, refusing—shooting rays of vision out all sides of me, like a planet or transmission, a magician in the universe, and I shut off, forever, a piece of my race.

616

I've stopped thinking about naked women so much. Something fundamental inside me is shifting. I used to think continuously of them, and when married seized my wife through a dream to awaken inside her—often. Now light beams break through holes in my mind, like rotted cloth. They were a comfort and distraction, naked women looming before my eyes, sharpened me one way while dulling me another, such that I cut myself on my own whetted flesh. Oaf! What is happening? Is my brain migrating north from the center where it was small but lethal, for now I seem utterly listing, diffuse? Am I crawling into my mind? I think of moles in their long gestation underground, finally emerging into light. I think of their blinking amazement. I am equally amazed and dampened. I know not what to think about! I loathe politics. Philosophy's too immense. I haven't the lunacy to speculate on the cosmos. Naked women have been my specialty; now they're evaporating. There's just a colony of holes before my eyes and dazzling light. I want to pull them back, my naked ones—their navels, midriffs, toes, breath—like an amputee wants his arm. What do you do when you're subject's gone? I was gourmand, connoisseur, master chef. My world's blank. I can't think of a proper topic to fill you with. At what point does a flower cease craving resplendence—those bromeliads, calla lilies, magnolias—salting the ground with brown petals? Is this a withering?

Am I a withering? Am I bleeding testosterone through
some psychic wound? Liquid yellow, gold? Am I
becoming woman? Am I dying—or chrysalis-like, being
delivered, finally, into something beautiful, the world
opening above my spine into a new profession of
love and transparency? I'm in transition. I'll wait
and see. All I know is my third wife's employer's ba-
by has captivated me—her baby smile, her spongy
cheeks, the way she grasps my finger, knee level,
and totters, chest out, like a queen. We go
shopping. All I know is unrelated disasters on the world's
other side wrench me. All I know is I'm not all fuck
and fantasy and man to naked women, braggart and
internally superior to my swarming rivals, and women
have transubstantiated into people. All I know is light
has crashed through some tunnel which dissolved, like
a wafer in its searing. Remember the little boy who
jumped in the milk and his crust of flour broke away
as he flew? All I know is something frightening and
sad is new and the word "screw" has broken into a
million pieces around my soul and bone structure.
When they loom now they are nude and embarrassed.

614

A bursting sun unrolls its morning flood through me.
Dipped in gold I scrawl love across this page. Suddenly
I am neither oblique nor mad, just a man in love with
his partner—meals together, talks, tandem sleeping,
the give and take of communion—the glint of gold over
everything. Lake in sun. Mirror. Water hovering
above cup's lip, like a cake of water. Today I will cook
oatmeal and wheat bran together, steaming, served
with milk, drink coffee opposite my lover whose hair
will be tangled still, from sleep, skin aglow before make-up—
we will discuss family finances and who will go to the bank
today about our loan, we will discuss my forthcoming
flight to Texas for my daughter's graduation, and her
graduation gift, we will mention the power of the
Red River and the North Dakotan flood, and perhaps
the Gingrich-Dole three-hundred thousand dollar loan,
the poverty of politics and politicians. The table, oiled
and rubbed from last night's company, will be drenched
in gold pouring in from the door. Our dead cells will
flake off us invisibly, will go about their dying, like a
secret comet's tail, beautiful to themselves, sparkling
off the core. Again the sun. It is a common day of exhaust
fumes and tempers, poverty and desperation, wealth
and arrogance, the usual explosive combinations, but
I am at peace, rising in brick oven-ness, loaf upon loaf
in my glowing soul, and know not why. Is just is. I
think of those images I have seen in photographs of
smelterers pouring molten steel into massive urns, how it
showers and splinters when it spills, and the steaming

veins and rivers flowing into molds—the men are poor and powerful, but full of pride, so it appears, and the steel they guide makes something strong. I feel like what they've made before it dries, still gold and red and brimming. If I am a beam shaped like an "I" to dangle from cranes above a bridge, that's okay; if I am the cage of a car, likewise. I am but a piece of things and my love a part. Today the counter aspill with grains glows gold under the window pane, each grain a boulder throwing a huge flame of shadow and I, without warning, awake from slumber's crumbling, am a heavy bowl, swaying and spilling.

605

I don't want to appear sentimental, but I've got to tell you
there's something about food that breaks my heart, something
about spoons and forks, pastas and beans, something about
the eating which wrenches the human being of me, the way
the biology craves food, the way it spirals on a fork, the way
it fills a cup and glides down tubes, the way it cools, the way
it steams windows and nourishes, the way it gives flesh to
bone, muscle to flesh, strength to lift. I am not religious but
when I sit before food at dusk—rice or enchiladas or greens
or polenta—I suffer a little for the cave between groin and chest,
the ghost, the hungry gift, the grotto of acids, fluids, blood,
enzymes, song, love, and greed, the stream of magma; how
we pull all day, hammer and grit, care, strain, sing, distribute,
need, navigate cars, featureless, like in-the-shell walnut meat,
compose, and hope. Our mouths wrap around sandwiches,
mayonnaise, lunchmeat, cheese, tomatoes, our fingers hold
the spoon of soup, like weight and counterweight, soft balances.
Brain knows, stored in some back cabinet, the crucialness
of food, knows the embedded panic button in the blood,
synonymous with the President's red phone, knows the
proximity of deprivation and fear, the threat of callousness;
but somehow the refrigerator is always full, as if replenished
inexhaustibly through the rear. Security! Forgetfulness! How
easy to reach for the tin of fish while plotting your next
slaughter on the market. Driveways, kids, and lawn chairs.
What breaks my heart I can't quite conceive—something to do
with tissue, thickness, continuousness, sponginess, ambition,
desire, pupils, the stretched-open hand, loneliness, children,
innocence, violence. Something to do with pendulums, opposites—

steel and down, fire and ice, night and light, rage and peace,
honesty and lies—but children most of all—adult and child.
Money covers food, food covers life, failure covers money—
paper, paper, scissors, knife. Something like that. Something
to do with grazing cattle, flipping tails, tufts of grass, blowing
leaves, cars whizzing by on interstates, the smell of dung and
prosperity, and the pendulum swooping back. I don't know. I
don't know. I keep envisioning the homeless with their placards
of distress at intersections beside traffic lights, dark humps in
ratty hats and parkas—Vietnam vets, schizophrenics, drug addicts,
blank stares, refuse, bodies like yours and mine, framed in bone,
wrapped by nerves; stomachs, lungs, livers, brains, parents,
kids, triumphs, failures, saliva, and tongues. That's not exactly it,
but the denial of it, the inoculation of work, the furious pre-
occupation of brain in the world, the arrogance of success,
the skin over sensitivity, the self-congratulatory soul on the
surface of the world in the plush of plentitude, the overpaid
aristocracy of President, Senator, Embassador, Head of State,
fatuous, on-the-take, duplicitous, transparent. The earth delivers,
keeps, inch-by-inch, pushing from its undepletable source an
ever-exchanging, imperceptibly giving off—like the tips of flames
or the ends of comet tails—nutritive thrill of potatoes, lettuces,
legumes, seaweeds, citruses, grasses, plankton, and wheat which
hogs, cows, sheep, and fowl, and unbelievable fishes, munch, gulp,
cross-cut, and rip to become food on our plates, simple piles of
food; it's not the brilliant nor the complex nor the cunning, nor the
lucky, nor the incessant yammerer at his desk, but the nobility of
food, the beauty of it, the pulsing hand, and the inalienable right to eat.

528

I tell the stranger sitting beside me on the plane which is
slanting in for a landing that I am going to rescue my
son from a psychiatric ward where his mother placed
him for experimenting with drugs and truancy, and the
stranger, a young woman, Born-Again, says, grasping my
hand and pressing her forehead against my arm, "May I
pray for him?" and proceeds to chant a most beautiful
prayer. She prayed as passengers filed by our side and
deplaned. The craft landed eventlessly and the visit with
my son was gut-wrenching and difficult. I brought him
home with me and, amazingly, he still lives! What we
cannot measure well we deify; Jesus is an immeasurable
commodity. My friend, long inexplicably depressed—
self-critical internal monologist, self-hating—worships
the serotonin reuptake pharmaceutical Zoloft, restores
balance daily, like a bath, to the immeasurable chemistry
of his brain. The twenty-four-hour-long self-regenerating
monologist dies, he says, at sunrise by the Marshall in the
pill—fast, deadly shooter. "I'll be on it for the rest of my
life," he adds. The great mysteries, the ones that over-awe—
Michelangelo's Chapel, Les Miserables, the Pyramids, the
microscopic gaps at human synapses: caverns we
fill with God to the brim, and over. How wonderful to
have glue to hold the whole together, clear, amber glue—
like bread—good, heavy bread to paste inside hunger.

511

I down the water hard, slam dunk it, really,
I'm in a hurry, skateboarding, sandlot ball,
little cellophane chest heart-heaving, little hands,
mother gaping—all my life I've been drinking
it, black rippled crystal in round glass, invisibly
saturating myself with its many psychedelic
permutations: Nehi, Coke, Jello, Popsicle,
lemonade, filling my cells, lining my bowels,
hydrating my eyes, and leaking it out me in
yellow arching streams through my urethra—
human fountain—collected it in plastic jugs as
Alaska's Fox Spring disgorged it up frozen
tubes, cupped and drank it from my palm raw
off mountain veins, boiled and cooled it in
the woods, from my own arms licked rain,
and of course the million spigots, fountains,
and hoses. Scientists say, in nineteen-ninety
six, that they are searching for life on Mars
by searching for water; the poles, they say;
the electrolytes that fuel the battery of life.
Such dependency begs a torture—subjugate an
enemy by depriving water, control the water,
poison the water, provide only enough water
to keep them begging, destroy with water—
rubies for the haves and ashes for the nots, such
a tidy box. And it burbles from the ground
and sheets down air's windowpane—aquifers,
lightning, limestone, manna clouds—and we
aerate it and chlorinate it and defilthify it in

unimaginable processing plants nestled between
foothills or flat along highways blooming water
flowers or stretching alongside outskirting
rye fields for the billion billion mouths and
biological systems to imbibe, suck, and knock
down endlessly without God, mind, light or
eye—its consummate invisibility—like love or
parents or family or friends which evaporate in
the blazing sun or torture of unconsciousness.

499

There might have been a hurricane and I might
have been in the waves straddling my Hobie
and waves might have hammered shedding spiny
spume and the waves might have sucked and
lumbered and the sky might have hemorrhaged and
the wind might have head-ripped and the rattlers might
have curled on roof-tops and the crabs might have
dug under and the men-o-war might have risen and
fallen on wild horses and the sting rays might have
saucered and my parents might have raged and
my parents might have screamed to me from
the cliffside beside the pink mansion and my parents
might have spewed acid and my parents might have
struck and the mullet might have submarined in gray
schools and the sky might have blotted and I might
have left white hand-prints in the sheen and I
might have hung up in the lip and I might have
dropped down the face of a gray elephant and I
might have stood on my world of foam and I might
have flown, flown and my parents might have
disowned and my parents might have died and a saw-
blade might have ripped my mother's stomach and
a knife blade might have slit my father's side and
there might have been a hurricane and I might have
been young and I might have snapped my Hobie under
my arm and driven it to the sea and I might have
straddled it in the wind-hammered gray dangling my legs
in a bowl of sharks and I might have drowned or
been devoured by any number of things and I might

have heard my father's voice straining into the
wind like a crooked-flying bird and I might have
heard and I might not have acquiesced but
paddled further into the mist where the elephants
herd and the zephyrs whistle in the delicate ear
bones and I might not have ever come back to the
solid brick house to the thick cool room to the neat
clipped grass to the clean round car to the rose red
mouth to the sparkling new curb and my father's voice
originating at the cliff might have plopped finally like a
stone in the sea a thousand feet short of my hearing.

494

What was dinner time but a ship in a gale, the
table sliding fore-to-aft, the cables straining, the
liquids sloshing from cups, rocking side to side
and front to back, mother, father, daughter, son
the points of a cross over Formica, nightly, a gale
sending breakers to shatter the beams of the
ark, winds to rip down sails, swells . . . my father
caught me in mid-air leap across the table to knife
my sister, I saw her dead in my head, shouted
me down, and snatched the knife, my mother
snarled "more money" at my father who blew fire
into her hair, my sister shriveled into her shoulders,
like a scrawny bird, it was dinner in America
behind nice walls—meat, bread, butter, white
rice, Del Monte peas—unanalyzed, undivorced,
and unaborted; repression and her hostilities. My
grades were poor. I hated eggs. My mother
bitched. My father raged. I hated my sister. She
tortured me. The steak was tough. Too fucking
bad. Shut up or I'll give you something to cry
about. Go to hell. Monster! Bum! Dinner time and
the meal was us, we ate each other's livers out
when every White working male could afford a
strip of real estate and a body by Fisher, it was a
drum we made of the kitchen table whose reverberations
felt all night we shocked in motion by six o'clock.
It was a drum, an ark, a stage whose lights
clicked out, whose actors tattooed cigarette smoke
on boozy air, their makeup cracked; it was

the unintentional tragedy of blind optimism, the
middle dawn of TV—Sullivan, Caesar, Skelton,
Benny, California, Conoco—pumping into the family
brain primroses and promises it couldn't keep, it
was illusion outstripping reality across the
dinner table of the world compounded by the
usual human fragilities and the resultant dementia.
Yet, at my table one of us, at least, could split and
float above himself, a conscious balloon watching
the comical evisceration, mother, father, sister,
brother, braving the waves, securing the cups,
swallowing and forgiving, blaming and embracing,
who could see, bumping against the top left
corner of the room, the slow destruction of four
souls, the gradual erosion of joy or love or self-esteem,
or the just plain blessing of feeling right, and the
individual struggles in the boiling sea not to burble
under, and the occasional off-handed victories,
watching with his balloon face this happening to him,
too, while something unbreakable, immovable,
iron-solid inside cried, "but it is us, by God, it is us."

492

Without consciously knowing it I depended on my Daddy to go to work each morning and return each night with food on the table. I came home from screwing up at school each day—slouch, hot shot, practical flunkey with a smarmy face—to pork chops or prime rib and peas or potatoes and ice cream or tapioca pudding—I expected this as my birthright and unspoken due. And he did: slipped on his pants, uncardboarded his shirt, slurped coffee, two eggs, toast and every day went to the office, some sleazy vending machine affair full of weevils, machine guts, syrup bottles, money filth, and steel furniture, King Daddy of the Milky Ways. I can't imagine wasting life in such a hell, but, for the yelling every night at mother, he seemed to love it, left each morning, chest thrust, as if he were the heavy-weight champion of the world, and, in fact, he was a pugilist. And the corn boiled and the burgers fried and the ketchup ran and the sundaes tickled and Daddy came and went day after day, like a blurry shuffling of cards through a deck, nothing but a whir in the air as he whispered by, and I ate and ate, grew and wanted, and he was no god, but a brutal, unanalyzed, repressed man medicated to the nines, but I didn't care because I expected, like a butcher expecting blade and block to cleave the neck, like a workman expecting excavator and gasoline to move the earth, which is what, I guess, life is: blood of the slaughtered sluicing in streams and the earth puckering under gasoline. My daddy whom I love but don't like was one of these finally nubbed to family theft and common misery. And the other three mantises of the clan—mother, daughter, I—by the fact of

our aliveness and constant need pitilessly watched him, a
perpetual motion machine, speed until he became a smoothed,
muttering piece of insanity. What did I care so long as
cells divided, flesh grew, brain multiplied, jaw clenched
on someone's butt—I had my furnace to feed and it raged
into sex and beer and drugs and cars and Burger Kings and
disregard and little pieces of attitude, peel outs on Saturday
nights, the jammed-open Holley burning the clutch into a fusion
of junk—daddy at work, daddy at home, daddy pumping down
pills with his head full of cheeping open-billed throated and the thud
of an ax blade meeting the block through an anonymous neck.

429

The heart boils like a chicken part in broth—
gray, dull, tumbling in the pot, overcooked,
hard veins wrapping the meat. Imagine a dead
crustacean on the sea floor buffeted by tides.
The sadness of estrangements, the disso-
lution of mates, the stars indifferent above
houses of rage. I grin among my colleagues at
the coffee wagon wiping a spill or waltzing
the hall, "Hey there," "How's it going?" "Fine."
Nothing heavy nor true, nor is truth a virtue.
To confess to homicidal tendencies, to say,
"I loathe you," "I'd as soon kill you," "You
make me sick," "I don't want you any more,"
horrible veracities better left dumb-tongued.
The heart boils in the tub, having betrayed
boiled with egomania, a little smug pug.
No one loves it now, ghastly little prig, least
of all women it flayed. Prayer was created
for hearts boiling gray, "God all mighty,
omnipotent One, I'm suffering, succor me,
raise me from this slime-soaked sea, throw
a baby my way, gold-flecked, shimmering,
free, teach me that most ridiculous of
dreams: how to love." Even atheists mold
their clay to God occasionally. What does
it mean? What does clamped-tight life reveal?
The heart clenches, "Not me! Not me!"
There's rancor in my tone, a thread of anti-
apathy about how I threw my heart in stew,

plunked it among tubers and shoots to roll
murky through dangling roots. I claimed you.
We rejoiced in rooms. Our robes fell open
on naked truths. Our sweet breathing curled
through, curled through. And I cut the trove
into parts and scraped it raw into a cauldron.

419

Cut the tip of my finger slicing turkey
the day before your heart surgery, mon, my
memorial to knives and blood. Took four months
to heal and even then, tender, like a shuddering
bell. Mom and son, Jewish, hooked, a couple
of losers. The surgeon cracked you through,
sewed you up, now you're fine save for the
two long worms crawling chest and thigh. Now,
I've broken up with my sweetie pie, my
finger's fine, you're paddling the wading
pool, the sun's banging, and the sky's
some cerulean eye scooping us both, a shovel.
No girl's going to rise up—your prediction—
and slaughter me with a butcher knife, because
there's no girl, 'cept you, mom, with your
bristly beard. I give up. I masturbate to
your red toe nails. Not that I wanted you
to die but a little liberation theology from the
grave wouldn't hurt—did you know, PS, I was
the only family member to cry. Besides, you
bleed money and I want mine. I'm forty-five.
Our lives are joined by their garbage—you've
got Dad and I've got you. You refuse to die.
Look at the little wooly lamb from behind,
so cute, like the back of my head. Don't
swing me round for not even God understands
my face. Now, healed—my finger, your prolapsed
valve—the earth burned clean we walk upon,
I search the personals ads for a new victim:

fit, blonde, blue eyes, looking for romance.
Even monsters try. How ugly all this is
oozing from my brain, like pus. I'm ashamed.
But there it is. You have maybe ten years and
I about thirty-five and by god geraniums in
hot garages have done better, thus far. I press
planets in my eyes. I'm glad you didn't die
and that dad's, I hear, now holding your hand
(the guilt must be piled), but I'm going to
stick the claw end of my hammer into your
eye, somehow, and remove you, like a nail, though
it be my last bursting, boiling, emancipatory piece
of effort this side of the God Blow. That's all.

399

I like the feel of cutting fruit—the pinelike
crispness of an apple; the way juice from a Bosc
pear sluices along the knifeblade; the kiwi; ba-
nana; casava; mango; or cutting unorthodoxly
across orange section, like one shattering
windows; the way apricot rises and gives birth
along cold steel,—I am an animal,—the manipulation
of the knife in my fingers, the way the handle
presses along my palm, like a baby mouse or the
materialization of my mother's voice. See the
grapefruit rind split open like a cry and weep
its milky tears on the slender flash and divide
fully, its two round halves to the cutting wood;
the watermelon; the fig with its bag of seeds.
I could kill. I could bare the beauty of human
flesh to the moon, liquid red swirled with sil-
ver light, white of bone shot with blue. What
kind of monster might I be? The grape peel bursts
and yields its filament veins to pure air, del-
icate green flesh clear as amniotica. And the
explosions of taste, human milk shot from tough
nipples into the mouths of babes, their heads
receiving, pliable little legs dangling over
cliffs of air. I love the feel of cutting fruit, like
fingerblood, plum red, oozing through an accident.
There are the bodies of men and women lacerated
by car steel, bleeding beautifully, hanging from
fresh-torn hooks, like dead chickens,. There are
the opal bruises and the blackened eyes which

are rainbow blue and green touched with gold,
and iridescent. There are the colors of danger and
disaster and ultimate demise. The juices pop and
arc onto July 4th grass, fat and green, as Stars
& Stripes Forever outwardly spill. We are all
imperilled by our disease of wounds and wounding.
There. The tomato pours forth a flood like a
ruptured nose, and the raisin stops the flow. Mo-
ther, mother, when they wheeled you to the ICU
tangled in four heart-plunged tubes, you were sluic-
ing blood, fine long threads which looped in air
and recirculated back through one leg, and I was
your little boy again in sun-parched shoes crying,
"Mama, Mama,"—human fruit, both of us. The ac-
cident plows. We look up. We have broad chests.
The father waits. The mother knows. The children
sing. The baby rests. Under my hand, along the
knife blade, the fruit of the world trembles and
gushes forth its seeds and meat and sugars and hair
and pools and sheets and pattern and core, a plenti-
ful shell—a precious cave—which empties beautifully
and thickens my fingers, like a necessary disaster.

377

Like a field of soy beans the pets keep renewing themselves—
those who desire cat, dog, bird, turtle, fish, reptile
harvest, like itinerants in a sweltering blaze. And the little
ones squeal and whine and cheep and cuddle, like teacups
full of Hershey's and mallows, and totter like fur balls, or crane
prehistoric necks through reticulated shells, scimitar beaks
shredding the lettuce, and pieces of poop squiggle out their
butts onto the rug, or squirt into the tank like bits of All
Bran, and the children giggle as hamster travels in its plastic
ball across the floor like a performing bear, and tails wiggle,
and teeth tear, and fishbone claws rip, and bellies slither,
and one infant lizard clings to a wall like Spiderman, and
all the Christmas babies peek from their boxes through big
fluffy ribbon and chew at the bow round their neck, and
leap their whole sack of guts into the air like jubilant
soldiers, and all of them—tortoise shell or brindle or tabby
or piebald or miniature or standard or shorthair or silver-
point—nudge their bowls, crunch, tear down through wet
pink tubes tasty strings of God, while the old bearded,
sagging, ragged, arthritic, glaucomatous, stroked out, senile,
toothless ones alive beyond their biblical ladder, arithmetically
computed in human years, explode on stairs, stiffen by
walls, weave through rooms, retrieve in dreams, copulate
in visions, bloat in bedrooms, fall off ledges, and lie
horrifically in corners with their limbs stuck out like road-
killed deer. Babies leap on the spot they once warmed with
their gray engorged bellies, rehabilitate the acres of air
they once invigorated. Claws of the dying curled under like
ram's bones drag along pavements behind red leashes.

See them die sweetly, adoringly, with snouts in our hands, or desiccated heads pathetic as a cob webs. For every two bushels of the deceased or dying a wall of newborns rushes forward packed with spiky face of spider monkey, scaly face of iguana, slender face of salamander, rottweiler, Angora, Chihuahua, angelfish, tarantula, cockatoo, Siamese, bluntnose milkshake, bottlebrush of ferret, French lop-ear, anemone, squid, angel-fish, the entire fluffcloud of the puppy kingdom, and every couch-shredding, flesh-pricking, god-slashing, eye-slitting cuteness of feline architecture in this contemptuous world. The wall rushes forth like a veined ocean muscle, spilling animals into our gaping caves the instant Old Faithful's heart breaks like a dam of unqualified adoration in his manger-bed. And your mother dies like a sheen upon the sea, and your father bursts like a goat spleen, and the surgeon cracks the sternum of your therapist, and locusts eat the cerebellum of the anthropologist, and sixty-eight blip off the radar screen, and Guinevere is raped, strangled, and rolled into a garbage bin, and the channel glasses over the ferry boat, and your grandparents fingers turn to rot-iron in the sod, and each of us tilts our head toward the great blistering ball while the surging wave of a wall cleanses the surface of the earth and delivers the waiting whelps into our hands.

370

If I could stick my tongue through the fat portion
of my palm, completely through so that it waggles on
the other side, like a worm or a soft sword; there
I would find God: an ordinary tongue, an ordinary
hand, but an extraordinary moment—a tongue penetrating
the soft lips of a hand which water-close around it
when withdrawn. God would be there—I am certain—
where the flesh gave way to the wetness, where the
little opening parted for the rooting tip, magically.
This fertile garden in the palm of a hand is where
the true sanctuaries on earth reside; where priest,
deity, and prayer converge in one act of privacy. The
tongue is sweet, like an apricot; the hand salty,
like a sea; and the tissue and blood within the hand
are thick, sticky and pushing, like a wall. I think
of joists and hinges, bolts and headnuts, but here
there is no grinding, gouging, nor dust of saw. It
is almost sex. There are sacred places—grottoes—
where self collides with self sans robes and hymnals—
where the red mouth of a dog breathes in dusk, and
the jewel of a wildcat's eye flares. Try it in your
tattered clothes, in your destitution-cell, with ash
smeared on elbows, and love gone mad. If I could
stick my tongue through the fat of my hand—there's
a blue crab clamped to my heart, a blue crab is
clamped to my heart, something leapt on me at birth
which was blue and hard and it clamped to my heart,
my heart wears the lid of a blue crab shell, the
first three beings I laid eyes on were my mother, my

father, and a broad blue crab—if I could stick my tongue through the fat of my hand, like a sun-slash through sky, without anyone noticing, in the solitude of my room, God would appear, like a sea floor after the moon draws up the gown into its globe. There's a knife and there's the robe and there's the secret soon beneath the robe. The hand splits and the palm becomes lips, eye, vagina, and the entering tongue self-love flooding. We all crumble a little inside. If I—if you—could pass material through itself, your fists might unrage, letting milk pour in. Raise your hand to your lips, finesse your tongue, in your mind slide it through.

355

I've taken flight like a flashing colorbird,
quick-winged, darting for the greening foothills,
over the speartops and the greenblades, whirring
like some kind of tissue machine, sweetly
into the Blue-Blue; scarlet-streaked, emerald-
swathed, golden-topped I am; Tinkerbellbird
hovering into the honey tube, beak-dipping,
streaking for red trumpets, and climbing, fruit-
fueled—cantaloupe, nectarine, blackberry,
apricot—light-like, flitting on slumberjoy,
flush with iridescence. Within my atmosphere swirl
the computer, the MasterCard bill, the antiseptic
tube, Fresca and her contemporaries, and the
shrapnel shell turning nebula-esque about
my chest—hefty things stuffed with wheels
& gears, which I, birdily, could scarcely lift. Mama
stardusts up with me, like a wake, Daddy sparkles,
and babies Milky Way as I flash & flit—birdboy,
hummerman. You'll know I've been through by
the trembling bluebells, the shivering feeders,
and the bulleted aspen leaves. No waxwinged
Icarus—dilettante!, experimental boy!—woozy with
arrogance elevatored to his dripdrip, I hover, spin,
wheel, catapult backward (split-tailed), bow, and
burrow into the honeypile, like the court jester
booming on rocket fuel—now that I couldn't care
less, now that life's nowhere, now that earth's
exposed itself as a helmetful of . . . HA! . . . now that
I know The Secret—which I'm not revealing—though

it involves the fact that Dreams mean nothing,
money is immaterial, science is a bit of flat-
ulence, the family is a cup of fog, and your
favorite tree—the one spray-painted green on
your brain—isn't. I wrap my arms around "so what,
big deal" like a hippo-big soap bubble, and
suddenly I'm shooting nimbus-ward, skydrilling,
midair halting, tail feathers ashovel. Slim Pickens
slapped the sides of The Bomb with his hat as
he rode it down, his life gone mad—a symbol of
The Recognition—and I roll, soul-blown, free
of relevance, fuck it all—it's okay, it's
unbelievably fine, it's not important anymore,
or even real—nevermind what—we all abandon Daddy
in our own way—bye-bye. And this particular
day I'm vibra-happy, punch-silly, and ecto-stunning,
and I'm borne on air, effortlessly, in full skeleton.

348

In the penis colony the men lounge in overstuffed
chairs near the hot buffet talking statistics
and percentages. The ceiling cathedrals and
the sounds are carpeted. Pipes of pin-stripes
stove their legs, socked and gartered in Bergdorf's,
and a signet ring corsets every third piggy. In
the penis colony the chef stuffs an apple between
guilt's snout, bakes it pink and blade-succulent, and
serves it in a glaze of shame sauce. All goes down
easy through the gullet of rage. "What say we have
a game," one suggests, all cheer, the mansion rocks,
and they pull out a gorgeous one from the stock
room: sexy-wet, fresh, full blush, cotton blouse,
untouched, adorable. Her little lungs heave.
"A blonde!" one looking like Mr. Monopoly Tycoon
shouts, and in a swarm the sport ensues. One
tenderly, upon his knees, proposes matrimony, hee!
hee! hee!, another lays down, as if over mud, his
glistening coat, deeply bows, and another pours
her a pink champagne while the face-blacked one
posing as the butler bolts the door. Then, one
plucks at her: a hair, a brow, a titty-tit-tit,
and getting very hot, all chime in. A welt of blood
back-floods and surges through the stump as one rips
off her apricot ear, three or four firmly plant
shoes and tear out an arm—have you ever seen
that gristle and bone rainbow in the baked chicken
leg?—and fall to, eating, one gouges out a gold-
flecked eye and pops it, like an egg, and several

wishing on a side, split her in two by the legs.
And the ritual begins: out come the knives. The
President gets the liver, the Vice President the
spleen, the Treasurer the bladder, the Secretary
her pancreas, the Sergeant-At-Arms both kidneys, and
to the members, the loyal members go the intestines
(both king and queen), the uterus, the pancreas,
the fallopian tubes, the eggs, the bladder, the sails
of the lungs, the brain, the lips, the slab of the
tongue, the esophagus, and all the scraps, a feast
beyond the believable, while outside under the
sweltering glow, along the skeleton of the city,
glide the oblivious commuters in glossy steel
bubbles. Afterward they scrape clean the
counter. Her heart they throw to Fi-Fi the poodle.

345

Oh Popsy-baby, let me have myself straight from the
palm-open of your heart, delivered like a pearl on
an oyster tongue, let me have my surfer hair to flip
sidewise like a cock-butt, let me have my indolence—
I'm 13 big ones and an individualist. Don't flush
the toilet on my head. Oh Daddyboy give me my blood
sticky & red to fling into my flesh like a string,
my blood-your blood without unleashing that red scream,
"Grow Up!" Daddyhead stop working so much and catch
my ball screwily flung into your mitt. What's so great
about a cigarette machine in a beer joint, that cold
green steel and quarter spill, filthy, slick? The
little money sack? Oh Daddyfuck put your bristly
mouth-beard over my snail-lips and give me mouth-to-mouth
in the parking lot, my head slunk back 'cause I'm yer
come mixed with mumby-egg. Draw me a map, let me
scrap with a handful of dollarfilth and a rustbike,
free like an emancipate in the seawind, hair blowing
in a whipfest and tan laying on, 'cause you don't care
if your boy's himself in his sandy blown town, with
An Attitude, you've applied artificial resuscitation
and his lungs 'r pumpin' in his cellophane membrane,
you bet cher life, your son by God full of Bar Mitzvah,
hamantaschen, and himself. Oh daddybum don't blow
brains out like yuv yapped about off & on again, rather
lunge and tackle me shoulderpadded with the tucked
in pig. I'm going fast, like a tinderfire
enveloped in ageflame: acne, facehair, full bush,
headed for goneness but for a burnmark on the

pinefloor. See the firepit of my loins. See
my branches flame. Then I'll be the lotus opener
and you'll be petrified in rage, old prunepit, canyon-
pile, dungstone. Old fathermine. Don't do it.
Don't pop those cockpills all night in their pill bins,
so coffinesque—diazepam & sleep hammer—nor cuddle
EST like a shock-junkie, no, go, for me, into the scare
house on the hill of your psyche, find the killers,
cry, shatter teeth, fling on the lights and make them
fly—bats—cloud of fears into the sun-strike bleeding
dry and white, so that you & I might, Daddypot & boy-
tyke, dance our feet stinging on this dazzling rind. Please.

228

And when I pulled a ribbon fish from the deep—
my God, it looked like a lethal umbilicus—
my father shrieked, "Look out, a shitsky!"
and he ripped the rod from my wrist so I would not get
sliced by its teeth. It shimmied and flicked,
brilliant snake, like a strip of razor wire,
flinging blood and silvery waterdrops everywhere.
But the pliers came, needle-nose, and down crushed
the foot over its flattened length, and my father
ripped out its guts with the treble hook and flung
it back into the blue-green deep. Stunning beast,
primeval, head full of teeth, instinctively darted
down like a sunbeam, before dying. On the deck
its blue-red throat, slime, clots of gore, a slash mark
were all that remained. The boat rocked in the sloughs,
like a cradle, and a pelican stared indifferent as a rock
as the clouds sailed by. And then later under the hammer
sky, I shrimped my hook, waited, my lips parched and
un-soda-popped (we drank them dry), my baseball cap shielding
my Jew eyes, I hauled up a dogfish, spiny, dangerous,
useless, tough; it bloated, croaked, dared me to touch
its urchin spines. He came again, this time gloved,
ripped the pole from my hands and, grabbing the line
three feet above the fish, like a sling with a stone
tied to the end, bashed it against the side of the boat.
Swung and bashed, swung and bashed, the dark weight
hooked in the throat-bones hanging on to this hellish
ride. But soon its tail began to explode, like plastic
strips, flying apart, pieces spiraling through

the air, gray and pink, sticking in its own black
blood to the prow, and then, its sides frayed and
split, spikes and needles spewing outward, like exploding glass,
its body slammed into a pulp, until finally it slid off
the hook into the grave of its birthplace. All that
remained of this Shylock fish: blast marks, black spots,
whip burns, where it hit and hit the side of our
ship. I stood like an emperor in his Colosseum
and watched. Sea wind parted my locks, sea gulls
swooped, and little pools of water soaked
my feet. It's not profound to say the great ocean
swallows its dead, like a mother, sealing the
wounds they make sliding in. After the pink and blue
ripple, the violence, the splatter of guts, a mirror
closed over the wound and the back-sloughs shone,
quiet as glitter. There is a craft skimming over
cold water, an Evinrude, pieces of raw flesh and
cutbait, an aerator sparse with shrimp bits, tackle
boxes, rods, reels, bloody hands, gaff and fish net,
boatsides nicked and cut, curved, like swan wings,
and a boy and his dad gliding over radiance toward home.

203

The desire to weep overwhelmed him, he felt the little facsimile of himself inside already flooding the plains with tears, he carried this sobbing effigy to business meetings, the club, the dinner table, the toilet where he sat over the tranquil pool, like a god. He felt the inexplicable need to surrender his life in a torrential rain, feeding the fronds and roots of trees, the climbing vines, the blossoming fields, huge drops clinging to leaves like a panther's eyes. This might be the ultimate mission of humankind—to gather and break, like a thunder cloud, to grow frail, to fall on concrete amidst passersby and almost die of humility. There the pungence of flesh would rise, like a burst overripe pear, seeds tumbling in bald fertility. There the stubbly or sun-devoured face tilted like an orchid gazes from cement. Oh, the need to cry, simply cry, shoulders quaking, groans escaping like a flock of grackles, overwhelmed, and yet he owned a Spartan face. Nothing broke nor would break from that stoic face. He wanted to wring his heart like a sponge, to grasp the engorged softness inside and squeeze it through his stolid eyes, to equalize the despair within to the productivity without. And how might he accomplish this? How does the captain in his deep sea craft also stand in water, symbolizing how nothing has gone as planned: not parenting, marriage, compassion, happiness, nor worldly gain? He wanted to howl with laughter, to rent films which split sides, sardonically; perhaps he could giggle himself to squalls, those poignant comedies scratched on celluloid that grip the soul. He thought of how, religiously, he watched sitcoms with his son—Meredith Baxter Birney, Phylicia Rashād, John Larroquette, Keshia Knight Pulliam all in a row on Thursday nights, the Quasar cozily flaring, his boy's doughy hand lightly touching, and he almost cries. He pushed down the knot. He thought of those chopped steak dinners out with his grandparents at the Night Hawk Café and how they listened and talked, and a mastodon lumbers up his throat. How impenetrable granite is, obelisks, court houses, monuments—low, stout, solid, unforgiving and how rain streaks across their veins. He considered punching himself into yielding, yielding, pummeling his thigh, or ramming his gut into a table edge; he imagined he could gouge out sorrow like jam from a jar, slurp it like a bear. He bites his thumb but no tears well. Is this what hell condemned males to: hardness, rage, isolation, fear, competitiveness, aggression, dictatorialism, a short nationalistic fuse? He knows a man who inserted his hands into a dog's mouth and ripped its head in two. Thank you! Thank you! He is not amused. He knows it is there, the devouring magma pool. He wants to disperse on the floor like a neglected burned Kool and weep for God knows who. He wants to peel layer-by-layer a brick until its inner hankie drools, to unravel rods, blocks, and slabs to the hills of raging within. His lover knows, his lover knows that worlds whirl in him as if in an amethyst; galaxies showering hues. He yearns for just one square foot of vulnerability, of dissolution, of immobility, one scalding hour of disintegration. Let us lament, he hears himself say, the human response to catastrophe which leaves one orderly, constricted, and afraid; the monolithism of beliefs which creates masonry; the wide tight band squeezing the kidneys; the fact, dismayingly, that no tear stains this page.

137

I want to pour children, like a pitcher of water,
through the hallways of my company: waifs, urchins,
gamins, orphans, brats, prima donnas, toddlers in
diapers, darlings of the upper-class; to roll them outward,
like a basket of eggs, from which individually
they would burst, whole and adorable. What a
mountain breeze that would be. What an exhalation.
To see them shrieking through the halls: the bow-legged
babies, the mischievous grade-schoolers, the lawless
pre-adolescents hole-punching the memo pads, defacing
the fax machine, dancing with in-boxes on their heads.
Primitive energy in this stale old hospital, like
the pulse of jungle drums. There in Matthew's office
Frederick pounds dumpling fists, wads Scotch
tape, coos fresh policy from his pouch of sweet
breath, and poops the Presidential chair. And little Sally
dirt-smeared, direct, and dictatorial pontificates
from Spencer's air. From outside our structure would appear
a bastion of multi-national efficiency, but inside
Justin would be yanking Debbie's hair, Chloe dumping
client files, and a barnyard of pigs, chickens, goats,
and hogs frolicking on the plains. Yes, I want to
reconstitute my office because I am sick of this
stiff-back sitting, this wrecking of spontaneity,
this snuffing of the soul. We were elected to be
their mentors, not their subduers. Let them miss the
urinals by a country mile, let them glop the rubber
cement. It's not a matter of disrespect, but of
keeping unpetrified. And I'm not an insurrectionist.

I want to loose a puddle of children from my palms, like
a genie who's scooped fertile mud: an ooze of hearts
jumping, a tadpole-like whipping through the
meticulous rooms. Sharpen pencils to the nub, bawl
for mother in a blast of honesty. We have failed
with our bright red pop cans, our cell phones,
our steroidal meat. We have served up hell in the
guise of success. Are you ashamed or is your pride
too steep? Have you been so inculcated that you can't
find the seams? Did you father's fist seal your brain,
and your mother's screams? Can you rebuild the citadel?
I want to release them, like a spasm of sea lice,
en masse, agglomerated, bricked-together, who are
abandoned by divorce, dragged screaming by the wrists,
criticized, beaten, taught lessons, sexually abused,
exploited, desolidified, in horrible times flipped in
the air, caught on saber blades, and occasionally loved;
to see them burst through the doors, explode into joy,
bubble the atmosphere, oh, seed the labyrinths! Until then
I will ache for the crack in the core which lets them in.

135

Afterward, he wondered about the enormous and complex
connectedness, the intertwining of tendrils delving
deep into the ground, the DNA spiral of love and histories
plunging into dark loam their inextricable root systems
of dependencies and desires. He thought of the apparent
simplicity of cows, sweet, brown-and-white spotted Holsteins
who mount each other in open fields, multiply, and low;
who shake their necks and wander off into valleys
stupid and indifferent. He stared at his chock full
bookshelves, the multi-colored spines of novels and non-
fiction, the encyclopedias and dictionaries, the OED, the tome
titled, "Dissection of the Vertebrates," and wanted to hide.
The blinds rattled from a mountain breeze as he lay
with her—cactus needle, aspen leaf, and cottonwood spume
fragrances filling their dusk-rich room. How huge, he pondered,
are our heads, like great glass globes scrimshawed with
complex geographies and delicate intricacies. They bang
against one another on ordinary strolls through public streets,
cracking at times, like fault lines. Pride straining
the faint capacity of weak necks. Afterward, he gloried
in the rich confusion of being human, the intermixtures
of love and reticence, the textured knowledges, the almost
infinite possibilities. His eyes rolled, like sparkling
marbles, wobbling to the source. He felt so blessed he wanted to
prick his finger to see the dark blood. He wanted to suck
his toes to feel the pillow tongue. "Contours," he thought,
the word "contours," "curves," "sensuality," "bones," "tendons,"
"knees," "words." The unfathomable alphabet of longing, the
refusal to stop wanting. This is life. Wanting is life. His

penis felt cold surrounded by air, by the room, the breeze
drawing across it, like water. He thought of the agony of his parents
in Texas, in Corpus Christi— "Body of Christ." How his father,
paranoid, guilty, and ashamed bruised his mother, knocked her
onto cold bathroom tiles; how he pops his pills. So beautiful
and tragic. He felt like a fish quivering on a hook. He
thought of beautiful diners at outdoor cafes, under the shadow
of mountains, sipping coffees, flicking sandaled toes, and
speculating on the attributes of future lovers. How gentle
the bed sheets felt on his face—floral and new—as he lay
with his palm tucked under her thigh and his toenails brushing her
foot bones. What landslides fall within the skin, what acts
of confusion. Clear, his love for her, unquestionable—that is
not the issue—but life, like rock, pulls down. "What did you say?" he
blurted, but she had said nothing. He thought that if he
could retrace his life back to the fork, back through
the tree-and-leaf-crowded path to the critical point,
and progress anew . . . but that would be false and suicidal.
He would lose the one woman he loves. How packed hard
the earth is. "Oh" he thought, "what a plethora." Where
are the cows lumbering on simple femurs to the lovely slaughter?
He looked at his watch and it was 7:15. Afterward, he felt
the dark dilation that normally accompanies him, the flooding largeness,
the pool of ecstasy and blurred boundaries. Populations of
women and men bled into his pores, like trickling fords,
like finger lakes, and settled in his heart, as he bled
through them. Lost borders. Stretched head. Melted. But
focused, too, and sharp as steel. The contradictions. The
conundrums. If skin had pockets he could have slid notes in
to calm himself after the water rushed away. The baby wriggling
in its crib. The mother's throat. The easy sleep. Afterward . . .

after what? . . . fusion? . . . union? . . . coitus? After breaking apart
he thought of the swerve on ice, the soundless slide,
life turning sidewise on its axis. He thought not about
loss of control but the inexorable fact of motion. And once again
cows appeared in his dreams—heavy, docile, dumb, and,—
oh, what does he know of cow, cow love, cow sadness, cow joy,
cow complexity? They lumber head down, chests sagging, bones
sticking out, like scaffolding, burdened perhaps with the failure
of the world. Dispel this myth, man, of omniscience. All
he knows is that he loves the woman, that she fills him, that
he's loved by her, that he was born sticky and wild through
his mother's loins, that life seems like a black-ice skid
sometimes when he shuts his eyes. All he knows is what's
in the declension. Afterward, all his variables in unison sang
of the clear, hard realities: the lamp, the desk, the
chair, the bath tub, time's fine blows on the sun-thickened
window sill. Of those he sang,
and of life's spectacular uncertainties.

114

I want to be shoes you slip into,
little dark bowls sleekly you fill,
skiffs that hug heels, the smell
of skin, leather, you—shoes the
shape of birds flown into when
you awake, or the gloves of a ballet
dancer toes entering me like food.
Shoes of the simplest type, heels
flat, lines cracked, mouths two hungry
pools, shadows imbued with sun-
spools. The body and its many
hollows: behind the knee, in
the cheeks, small of back, pocking
the wings, in my shoulder blades
so deep they could gather rain,
and the insteps, like sandstone
caves you could fill by pouring
in your soles. I want to be your
mold, thinly coating you like oil,
the walls of a calve's skin dam
that take your shape flowing in.
A skin against your skin I would be
pliant, flexible, adherent, alive
within which the flame of you
might rise through your mother's
tomb, your daughter's brain,
your eldest son's tenacious ad-
diction, your ninety year old
dad's dead violin. Pour into me.
Stand up in me like living crystal.
I . . . I . . . I want to be—O, such grandiosity—
just something comfortable.

40

Loneliness is an interminable suicide
in which nobody dies;
the hives of blood, bone,
and spiraling chromosome
thrive in the exquisite mansions
of mud, terminals
through which sticky traffic flows
bearing its rich and precious cargoes.

Loneliness is an illness
which refuses to kill,
leaving all vital organs alone
in their inexpressive respirations:
nails grow, lungs exchange,
and if you are male
seed whirls in its milky home.

But something essential,
indefinable,
under the lungs, under the weighty
aortic hose,
in the primal loam,
where hope is sown, and joy,
a delicate sinister cabbage grows—
crowding insides out pores,
sores, and the brilliantly
functioning capillarious nose

in red-blue filaments,
like spatter of a freshly slaughtered
lamb or kid over
the precipice of a bed
converting the room
into a killing floor.

"I shouldn't have dumped him."
"I should never have skipped out."
"What an idiot I am."
"I should crawl on my knees."
"I require too much."
"Christ, I'm fucked up."

Loneliness is a pistol that won't discharge,
just aims and aims
with its hammer and shells
causing through the parapsychological hole
causing floods of this second blood
through a psychological hole
to rise over the table tops
in eddies and swirls
and to keep rising . . .

26

To lay a sheet of light over a sheet of dark
over a sheet of light over a sheet of dark
like a pastry formed of filo dough, light,dark,
light,dark,light,dark until the whole personality
is included, sadness over joy over love over shame,
to lay sheet over sheet of flaky delicacy
so easily hurt and devoured, yet so delicious.
And there you are gorgeous and valuable and
acquiescent and whole whose feet stand you up,
and smile snaps you level, and hope pulls your
great frightened mass of aliveness through the world,
and fear shoves you back, and obstinacy leans
you forward into the claws of the wind, and
beauty sears your eyes into the fire of desire
("Holy shit!" he mutters about a stunner in
his vision), and grief sits you down on your ass
like a boulder, and jubilation flings your blood
into the circles of the air, and greed grabs need
and rips out throats, and joy electrifies toes
into dance, and rage explodes your breast
like a mushroom cloud in reverse, and agape
flattens you into an inner-planetary hug, and lust
returns you into a bullet splitting air,
and tenderness hurls you over-the-falls,
and love,love,love alternately reconstructs you
stronger and cracks your bones one by one—
the cartilage in your nose, the match
sticks of your fingers and toes, the bell house
of your skull, the chalk of your thigh bones,

the brittle timber of your ribs, and packed sand
of your hips—all crushed like a ruby-throated
thrush under the enormous closing pressure
of the valentine fist. So go easy, be kind
to the oozing baklava, the popover, the puff-
pastry stuffed with blueberry, blackberry, almond,
or pecan; the spinach and feta strudel
wrapped in buttered gauze; the deep-dish
pie steaming from the oven, bubbling, tantalizing,
gold around the edges with a yielding heart. . . .

24

The daily vigil of the heart maintains
locked in its high bone tower of unexpiring love,
revolves, pierces, fixes in its gaze
the flashing green or red being of its need,
misses nothing that it has the power to perceive,
like the eye of the eagle, steady, clean flaring
it the tall white undespairing turret of its life.

The daily vigil of the heart, pure, relentless burning
into the rich, perpetual plenitude,
the textured weave of branching bloodstream
and pomegranate lives, identifies its desire,
like the unquivering arrow peeling back the air
flying true to its mark when released
by the steadfast hand of doubtlessness,
another Apollo among the ruins.

(How pretentious my language has become,
Byzantine, Baroque, ornate, obtuse. I'll try again.)
High in my cage of loneliness when I was but

a heart-sized eye I met the woman of my desire,
slight, pornographic, playful, alive, smart
as an ineradicable snake-bite and confused as a toss
of unloaded dice, comfortable in lacy black and
raven-red tights, and I knew in my cold bower of need
that I must have her—and that I shall—and so
I gave her access to my heart, those remote chambers
which permit me to fuck, support, comfort, and stroke

and slide into her parental house to suck the bones
of delicate thighs and read her work and engage
her two bratty boys—those dysfunctional screamers—
and drive her through blizzards into dazzling light
and adore and reveal and cry and hope
and wrap in the welcoming wetness of my heart—

but she loved another man, and I did not win.

1

I would like to go into the office next to mine
—it belongs to Dean, a kind, sweet man—
and just sit and cry. I would like to just
sit and cry, sit and cry without inhibition,
shoulders shaking and huge tears
rolling to the floor. I would like to stroll
into his office with its filing cabinets, calendar,
and bulletin board, sit in his client chair,
and cry for nothing and for everything.
"Love," I might mutter, "mountains," "children,"
dissimilar words pulled from a larger
and deeper phrase who meaning I have lost.
How nice it would be to crumble before a man
without shame or guilt, to curl into a sculpture
of pain and hopelessness and loose it.
As simple as a blossom widening before rain,
a man aware of his humanity.
I would like to go into Dean's office
for he is a kind, sweet man, no longer a boy
nor yet an opportunist and, solvent of bone, muscle
and curvature of skin
dissemble in a chair in the middle of the day,
to say in that soundless infinity underneath words:
understanding is emptiness, vision is puncturing,
and loss a bubble expanding in our hands.

Acknowledgments

The author thanks David Baratier of Pavement Saw Press and Che Elias of Six Gallery Press, as well as the editors of the following journals: *Another Chicago Magazine, Antioch Review, Artful Dodge, Chelsea, Confrontation. Connecticut Review, CV2* (Canada), *Cortland Review, Exquisite Corpse, The Fiddlehead* (Canada), *5AM, The Georgia Review, Green Mountains Review, Greensboro Review, The Harvard Review, Hiram Poetry Review, Iron* (UK), *Karamu, Malahat Review* (Canada), *Many Mountains Moving, Membrane, The New York Quarterly, Left Curve, The Literary Review, Old Crow Review, Paperplates* (Canada) *Pavement Saw, Penny Dreadful, Pleiades, Prairie Journal* (Canada), *Prism International* (Canada), *Quarter After Eight, Rampike* (Canada), *Rattle, Response, Tarpaulin Sky, Third Coast, Willow Springs, Windsor Review* (Canada), *Yellow Silk.*

About the Author

Gordon Massman divides his time between Medford, MA, and the island of Frenchboro, ME.